No one ever really cooks alone.

Even during our quietest, most solitary moments, preparing a meal inevitably stirs up recollections of meals shared with loved ones from our past. It is these valuable memories -- stimulated by our five senses -- that feed our souls and build legacies.

You Never Cook Alone

Stirring Memories, Feeding Souls & Building Legacies

A Cook Book

for

The Well Fed Family

Elise Johnson

Copyright © 2012 by Elise Johnson

All rights reserved. No part of this book may be reproduced by any means whatsoever without permission from the author, except for brief portions quoted for purpose of review.

Cover Designed by Emily Barahona
Photography by Marsha Pearce and John Lambeth
Edited by Jessica Martinez

www.cookingwithelise.com

ISBN-13: 978-1469952451
ISBN-10: 1469952459

For

Michael, Nathaniel and Alexander

I love you dearly!

Thank you for adding such immeasurable love, joy and laughter to my life.

May you continue to make memories in the kitchen and around the table!

Table of Contents

Acknowledgements, 13
Introduction, 15
PART I - EVENTFUL MEALS, 17

    IT'S MORE THAN JUST PIZZA, 19
        Basic Pizza Dough, 20
        Multigrain Pizza Dough, 20
        Fresh from the Garden Pizza Sauce, 21
        Mediterranean Pizza, 23
        Breakfast Pizza, 23
        Make-Your-Own-Pizza Night, 25
        Sweet Sticks, 26

    FAMILY GAME NIGHTS, 29
        Sloppy Joe Sliders, 30
        Sausage and Pepper Heros, 31
        The Great BLT with a Kick, 32
        Oatmeal Chocolate Chip Cream Cheese Bars, 34
        Chocolate Peanut Butter Oat Bars, 35
        Orange Vanilla Sugar Cookies, 37
        Cookie Baking Tips, 38

    UNDER THE STARS, 39
        Hot Cocoa with Peppermint Whipped Cream, 41
        Maple Wheat Cloverleaf Rolls, 42
        Spread the Love Spiced Carrot Marmalade, 43
        Warm and Hearty Minestrone Soup, 45
        Double Peanut Butter Chocolate S'mores, 46
        Southern Sweet Tea with a Twist, 47
        Trail Mix, 48
        Granola Clusters, 48

PLAYING WITH YOUR FOOD, 51

    Caesar's Tableside Salad, 52

    Homemade Fettuccini with Bolognese Sauce, 53

    Maintaining Your Pasta Maker, 55

    Roasted Vegetable Lasagna, 56

    Pasta Tips, 58

    Spaghetti with Sausage and Pepper Sauce, 59

    Sausage Ravioli with Brown Butter Sauce, 60

    Cranberry White Chocolate Biscotti, 63

    Lavender Almond Panna Cotta with Roasted Cherries, 64

MURDER MYSTERY DINNERS, 67

    Wholegrain Pan Rolls, 69

    Compound Butters, 70

    Caldo Azedo (Sour Soup), 72

    Mom's Portuguese Pot Roast, 72

    Pan Gravy, 73

    Carrot Potato Mash, 74

    Green Tomato Cake with Brown Butter Icing, 75

    A Medieval Mystery Dinner, 78

    Herb Buttermilk Biscuits, 80

    Creamy Potato Leek Soup, 81

    Sing a Song of Six Pence French Meat Pie, 82

    Flaky Pie Crust, 82

    Arroz Doce (Rice Pudding), 84

PANCAKES: STACKS OF FUN MORNING, NOON AND NIGHT, 87

    Homemade Whipped Cream, 88

    Mock Maple Syrup, 88

    Pumpkin Granola Pancakes, 89

    Wholegrain Apple Oat Pancakes, 91

    Blueberry, Orange and White Chocolate Pancakes, 92

    Orange Maple Syrup, 93

    Swedish Pancakes with Cannoli Filling, 94

    Chocolate Wine Sauce, 94

    Sweet Potato Pancakes Adorned with Spiced Nuts, 96

    Cinnamon Roll Pancakes, 98

CHINESE TAKE IN, 101
- Steamed Dumplings, 103
- Nate's Dipping Sauce, 103
- Fresh Lettuce Wraps, 104
- Chicken and Vegetable Egg Rolls, 105
- Tips for Making Egg Rolls, 106
- Family Fun Project, 107
- Asian Chicken Kabobs, 108
- Chicken Fried Rice, 109
- Fortune Cookies, 110
- Almond Cookies, 111

AN AFTERNOON TEA OR BRUNCH, 113
- Mom's Best Chicken Salad Sandwiches, 115
- Roasted Asparagus Quiche, 116
- Everything but the Kitchen Sink Breakfast Pudding, 117
- Strawberries and Cream Scones, 119
- No-Recipe-Needed Orange Glaze, 120
- Pumpkin Spice Muffins, 121
- Pumpkin Chip Scones, 122
- Peanut Butter Banana Muffin Tops, 124
- Berry Parfaits, 125

A NIGHT OF NOSTALGIA, 127
- Back-in-the-Day Wedge Salad with Thousand Island Dressing, 129
- Baked Cheeseburger Macaroni and Cheese, Please, 130
- Golabki, Stuffed Cabbage Rolls, 131
- Old Faithful Whipped Mashed Potatoes, 133
- Creamed Corn, 134
- Mom's Baked Pork Chops, 134
- Peanut Butter Milkshakes, 135
- Heavenly Chocolate Pudding, 136
- "Get Me a Man" Pie Story, 138

BIRTHDAY BASHES, 139
- Spinach Feta Turkey Burgers with Green Goddess Mayo, 141
- Grilled Lemon Chicken, 142
- Tortellini Salad, 143
- Party Beans, 143

Summer Potato Salad, 144

Hawaiian Cake, 145

Pecan Bars, 146

Mamma's Pecan Pie, 148

KLINGON BANQUET, 150

Romulan Ale, 151

Klingon "Heart of Targ" or Sesame Chicken, 152

Klingon "Gagh" or Noodles in Peanut Sauce, 152

The Generations Cake, 153

"Granny's Pineapple Cake" Story, 156

PART II - NO PASSPORT NECESSARY, 159

PORTUGAL, 161

Portuguese Kale Soup, 164

Vavo's Pan Fried Fish and Red Gravy with Stewed Potatoes, 165

Vavo's Stewed Potatoes, 168

Portuguese Stuffing, 168

Vavo's Spaghetti and Meatballs, 170

Malasadas, 173

Massa Sovada (Portuguese Sweet Bread), 175

The Significance of Folar da Pascoa (Easter Bread), 177

INDIA, 179

Naan Bread, 180

Chicken Tikka Masala, 181

Infused Basmati Rice, 183

Raita, a Cool Cucumber Yogurt Sauce, 184

ENGLAND, 185

Rustic Brown Bread, 186

Cottage Pie with Onion Gravy, 187

Mushy Peas, 189

English Bread Pudding with Caramel Sauce, 190

IRELAND, 193
    Irish Soda Bread, 194
    Irish Beef Stew, 195
    Colcannon, 196
    Traditional Irish Scones, 197
    Blueberry Peach Crumb Cake, 198

SPAIN, 199
    Asparagus, Potato and Onion Omelet, 199
    Spanish Salad, 200
    Chicken, Shrimp and Scallop Paella, 201
    Spanish Flan, 202

ITALY, 205
    Farro Cherry Tomato Salad with Goat Cheese and Lemon Pesto, 206
    Sausage Lentil Soup, 208
    Chicken Milanese, 209
    Cavatappi with Tomatoes and Garlic, 210
    Polenta-Cherry Cobbler, 211

FRANCE, 213
    Crisp Pear Blueberry Salad with Roquefort and Toasted Walnuts, 213
    Coq au Vin, 214
    Potato Puree, 215
    Berry Clafouti, 216

MEDITERRANEAN and MIDDLE EASTERN CUISINE, 219
    Hummus with Toasted Pita Chips, 219
    Al Motubug, 220
    Tabouleh, 222
    Greek Salad, 222
    Chicken and Spinach Spanakopita, 224
    Baklava, 225
    Kourabiethes (Greek Wedding Cookies), 226

JAMAICA, 227
    Creamy Jamaican Squash Soup, 228
    Jamaican Jerk Chicken Kabobs, 229
    Fried Plantains, 230
    Jamaican Rice, 230

Jamaican Cornmeal Pudding, 231

What I learned around the table, 233

The Benefits of a Well-Organized Kitchen, 235

Helpful Meal Planning and Money-Saving Tips, 241

Index, 246

With a grateful heart…

I sincerely thank those who made this dream a reality. While writing this book for my three men and for our family's future generations, I never imagined it would blossom into something others would want to read. Words cannot convey how very much I love my family and friends. I wish I could shout **"God, thank you!"** to the mountain tops! Thank you for blessing me with my husband, Michael, my best friend and my biggest supporter in life. Thank you for giving me the honor of being a wife to such a remarkable man who always recognizes what I can accomplish before I even know it or can imagine it myself. Michael, my heart is yours…forever.

Thank you for my two wonderful sons, Nathaniel and Alexander. The joy they have added to my life is beyond measure. Being a wife and a mother has been an absolute privilege. My three men make me a better person and constantly remind me that life is not about the destination, but the ride.

Thank you, God for my parents, Ed and Mary, who have always illustrated a strong work ethic and the strong principles of a loving and committed family. Thank you for providing me with a family who set a remarkable example of caring for others. How thankful I am for all of my dear, dear friends and for each and every person who has encouraged me in my life. Sister Eleanor, you were right. Although I couldn't speak I could write! Thank you for the encouragement you gave me as a child. I did it – I wrote a book!

To everyone who has encouraged me, THANK YOU! Each of you has impacted my life in so many ways. Thank you to Tony Arnold of Engage Media Communications for believing in me, in this project and in the mission of the Well Fed Family. I appreciate your attention to detail, your quality advice, your integrity, your diligence, patience and humor--even when I couldn't remember my left hand from my right.

How grateful am I for David Sanford and his willingness to invest his time in this project. Thank you, David, for providing much-needed guidance and most importantly encouragement. Thank you especially for reminding me to enjoy each moment!

I'm so grateful to my graphic designer, Emily Barahona, for taking such good care of my third "baby" and for being such a significant part of this incredible journey. The warmth of our family portrayed in the cover was the work of Emily, Marsha Pearce and John Lambeth. How very much we appreciate you all!

The person who helped my words dance off the pages was my editor, Jessica Martinez, who threw herself whole-heartedly into this project. For that, I thank her greatly.

A special thank you to my godfather and uncle George, who spent hours with me on the telephone helping me remember parts of my grandmother's recipes. It is because of your loving care that my children were able to walk into their great-grandmother's home just the way it used to be.

… My dear, dear Vavo, THANK YOU for seeing only my heart and for loving me unconditionally. I never cook alone because you are always with me…

No one ever really cooks alone...

Even during our quietest, most solitary moments, preparing a meal inevitably stirs up recollections of meals shared with loved ones from our past. It is these valuable memories--stimulated by our five senses--that feed our souls.

For me, the smell and taste of foods I once savored with my grandmother brings me right back to the comfort and sanctuary of her little basement kitchen. Recipes I used to enjoy with my own family transport me back to our early years, long before my boys became young men and left for college. The taste, sound, smell, texture and look of food constantly reminds me of those I love and the special moments and occasions that have made up our family's lives.

I originally wrote this book for my husband and children about five years ago. I wanted to ensure that my children not only had the recipes they grew up enjoying, but that they understood the importance of passing on a family legacy.

My childhood memories are filled with wonderful moments around the table, and no wonder. Our family table was the place where I felt most comfortable and most loved.

Due to a terrible speech impediment that reared its ugly head when I was four years old, I didn't speak with ease until I was about sixteen. As a child, stuttering made daily activities like answering the telephone, learning at school, and even saying "I love you" nearly impossible for me.

My parents were very supportive and sympathetic, and worked hard to pay for speech therapy and private schooling. My peers were mostly kind to me. Unfortunately, I still struggled with low self-esteem throughout my childhood. My impediment caused me colossal, almost unbearable anxiety each and every moment of my life – except in the kitchen and around the table.

During my childhood, our family lived in my grandmother's immaculately-kept three-tenement house in the city of Fall River, Massachusetts. My grandmother, who we called "*Vavo*," (which is Portuguese for grandmother) lived on the first floor. My father, mother, younger sister and I lived in one of the two apartments above my grandmother's home for many years.

Our family rarely went out to eat. My mother almost always prepared our meals, and saw to it that we gathered around the table each night for dinner. Around that table I mattered, I belonged, and I was loved. It was the one part of the day that I truly enjoyed. *There was so much power in that hour!*

I also cooked and ate frequently with my grandmother. It was she who would ultimately influence my love of cooking. Vavo spoke mostly Portuguese, and I hardly spoke at all. But we didn't need to talk–the special time we spent together in the kitchen formed the foundation of our relationship. After an arduous day of school, my grandmother's kitchen was a safe haven; a respite; **a *place where I was well-fed.***

Years later...

As a young woman I lived in my own little apartment, which was so close to the home I grew up in that a simple walk across the street kept Vavo and I doing what we loved together. It was while I lived in that apartment that I met my best friend and wonderful husband, Michael.

Feeding people has always been a central way for me to demonstrate how very much I care about and love them, and Michael caught on quickly. I guess you could say that I found my husband's heart through his stomach!

Two wonderful sons and many years later, our family still makes meals eventful. Time in the kitchen and around the table has supplied our family with more meaningful memories than I can share in one book.

Children who enjoy meals with their families learn how to communicate well and model loving behavior. They also get better grades, eat healthier, are more self-sufficient, build self-esteem and form a solid identity. When we feed our families, we don't just nourish their bodies. We nourish their hearts and souls as well.

I hope the stories within this book will make you laugh, cry and feel encouraged. Above all, I hope this book does more than help make your family meals eventful. I hope it helps you create priceless memories, fill your hearts and homes with untold joy, and connect past, present and future generations. ***I hope you never cook alone.***

PART ONE

Eventful Meals

Over the years our family has taken great pleasure in making our meals eventful. A little intentional planning and a lot of love have led to some very memorable meals, which we are now sharing with you.

Food is a powerful catalyst, and something every person has in common. Everyone eats! Food accomplishes something very few other things can: it brings people together. People bond with one another over the communion of food, regardless of language barriers, demographics, political views or religious beliefs. The phenomenon of food and our five senses connects all people and all generations.

People often ask me two questions: "What is your secret ingredient to success in the kitchen?" and "What do you think is the most important kitchen tool?" My answers are always…

LOVE is the secret ingredient and our **FAMILY TABLE** is the most important kitchen tool.

It's More Than Just Pizza

Basic Pizza Dough

Multigrain Pizza Dough

Fresh from the Garden Pizza Sauce

Mediterranean Pizza

Breakfast Pizza

Make-Your-Own-Pizza Party

Sweet Sticks

Today, Americans eat around 350 slices of pizza every second! There are more than 61,000 pizza parlors in the United States alone, and fast food pizza is a $30 billion industry.

I know it is very easy to pick up the telephone and order a pizza and, sure, it might arrive at your door within thirty minutes. But if you have yet to make your own pizza together as a family, you are missing out on a lot! The first time my husband and I cooked together we made homemade pizza. Before our children left for college, making pizza together once a week was a family tradition. The aroma of fresh homemade pizza filled our home every Friday night.

I first developed my Multigrain Pizza Dough recipe in 2003 in an effort to create pizza dough that was healthier and more filling for my family. Filled with whole wheat, oats and flax seed, this dough is not only superior in flavor, but full of vitamins, minerals and fiber, which will keep you satisfied longer.

If that's not reason enough to try this recipe, your family will have loads of fun preparing the dough, kneading it, stretching it out, and making the pizza "theirs" by adding their favorite toppings.

Basic Pizza Dough

1 tablespoon dry active yeast
1 teaspoon granulated sugar
1 cup very warm water (105 to 115 degrees F)
2 cups unbleached bread flour
¼ cup olive oil
1 teaspoon kosher salt

Combine the yeast, sugar, water and ½ cup flour in a small bowl. Allow the mixture to sit for about ten minutes so that it can proof. Once the mixture doubles in size, it should have a sponge-like appearance. Place the mixture in a larger bowl and add the olive oil, remaining flour and kosher salt. Stir it with a wooden spoon just until it combines, then pour it out onto your lightly floured island or counter. Sprinkle flour on top of the dough and then begin kneading. The dough should be sticky, but not enough so to stick to your hands. Continue adding flour little by little as you knead. The total flour used for this recipe should not exceed 2 ½ cups.

Knead dough until it is as smooth as a baby's bottom. Place dough in a large bowl that has been greased with a little olive oil. Cover with a dish towel and place in a draft-free area for about two hours, or until the dough has more than doubled in size.

Multigrain Pizza Dough

Makes one large pizza

1 cup very warm water (105 to 115 degrees F)
1 tablespoon baking yeast
1 teaspoon granulated sugar
½ cup old-fashioned rolled oats
½ cup whole-wheat flour
½ cup whole flax seeds
1 tablespoon olive oil
1 teaspoon kosher salt
1 ½ cups unbleached all-purpose flour, plus extra for kneading

Combine the water, yeast, and sugar in a large mixing bowl and set it aside until foamy, about five minutes.

Whirl oats in a blender or food processor until they are the consistency of coarse crumbs.

Once the yeast is thoroughly dissolved and frothy, add in the olive oil. Then add all of the dry ingredients. Mix them well until a dough forms. Turn the dough onto a floured surface and knead for 5 to 7 minutes until smooth and elastic, adding the remaining flour as needed.

Lightly oil or spray a large bowl. Place the dough in bowl, covering both sides with oil or spray. Allow the dough to rise until it doubles in size.

Fresh from the Garden Pizza Sauce

I find it extremely difficult to think anything but pleasant thoughts while eating a homegrown tomato. Homegrown tomatoes don't just taste delicious--they're good for you and very easy to grow. Whether planted in the ground, hung in a basket or placed in a large pot on your deck, tomato plants will provide your family with all the tomatoes you will need in a season.

Similar to cooking together, gardening together promotes family participation. Children are much more likely to try fresh fruits and vegetables if they help choose which plants to grow, assist in the planting, help nurture, water, and watch the plants grow, harvest them, and then head into the kitchen to prepare a meal or snack with their harvest.

Try preparing this super, easy and fresh pizza sauce while you're waiting for your dough to rise. Double the recipe and freeze what is left for your next pizza night--or for whenever you have a craving for homemade pizza.

2 tablespoons extra-virgin olive oil
1 small yellow onion, minced
2 garlic cloves, finely diced
4 cups peeled, seeded, coarsely chopped tomatoes
1 (6-ounce) can tomato paste
1 tablespoon oregano, crumbled
1 teaspoon basil, crushed between your fingers
1 bay leaf
1 tablespoon granulated sugar
1 teaspoon kosher salt
½ teaspoon ground black pepper

Puree the tomato chunks in your food processor or blender.

Heat the olive oil in a sauté pan.

Add the onions and cook them over medium heat for about 5 to 6 minutes, or until transparent. Add the minced garlic and cook another minute.

Stir in the tomatoes, tomato paste, oregano, basil, bay leaf, sugar, salt and pepper and bring to a boil. Simmer the sauce over medium-high heat uncovered for about 30 minutes or until thick, stirring occasionally. Remove bay leaf, then serve or store!

Basic Pizza Construction

Place the kneaded dough on your pizza stone or pizza pan. The dough should be soft and pliable. With your hands, press and flatten the dough, moving from its center outward, until it fills the pan evenly across. Make sure not to pull the dough.

Spread pizza sauce over the top of your dough. A little goes a long way; we use about ½ cup of sauce per pizza. Be careful when choosing pizza sauce--many commercial brands have a high sugar content. Making your own sauce is your best bet. However, if you don't have the time, choose a bottled tomato sauce without corn syrup and additives.

Sprinkle the mozzarella cheese evenly over the top of the pizza. Add your favorite toppings, then bake the pizza on the bottom rack of a preheated 450-degree oven for about 10 minutes. Finish baking on the top rack for another 10 minutes or until it's nice and crispy.

Mediterranean Pizza

We love making this Mediterranean pizza at home. It has become one of our family's favorite pizza recipes.

1 recipe Multigrain Pizza Dough
½ cup Fresh Pizza Sauce
2 cups mozzarella cheese
½ cup chopped spinach, fresh or frozen (squeeze out liquid if using frozen spinach)
1 plum tomato, chopped
2 cloves garlic, minced
½ cup reduced-fat feta cheese
¼ cup red onion, diced
¼ cup Kalamata or black olives, sliced

Prepare the dough and spread it onto your baking stone or pan. Spread fresh pizza sauce over the dough and add mozzarella cheese. Add all of your toppings and place the pizza in a preheated 450 oven for twenty minutes, beginning on the bottom rack until it's nice and golden. Move your pizza to the top rack for the last few minutes.

Breakfast Pizza

Oh, what a wonderful pizza for any time of day! I'd feast on this for breakfast, lunch or dinner. I especially love using chourico, a type of Portuguese smoked sausage, for this recipe.

Our family ate a lot of chourico. A blend of lean pork chunks and fine spices, chourico adds tremendous flavor to many dishes and is delicious all by itself. Found in many stores in my hometown of Fall River, Massachusetts, chourico and Pimento Moida, or fresh red crushed pepper, can be easily shipped right to your door. You may go to my website (cookingwithelise.com) for a list of stores.

For this recipe, I recommend ordering chourico, but you can use your favorite ham, bacon or sausage. Just be sure to cook and drain the bacon and/or sausage well before adding it to your pizza.

This pizza is beautiful, flavorful and easy to make. It tastes great anytime, but we especially love having it for dinner. In fact, we love it so much that I actually double the recipe and make two pizzas. We all look forward to enjoying it again for lunch the next day!

1 Recipe Basic Pizza Dough
2 small or one large red potato, sliced and boiled in salted water until just about cooked
½ pound Mello's ground chourico or your favorite cooked sausage
1 shallots, sliced
1 pint cherry tomatoes, with green tops removed
1 tablespoon olive oil
2 extra-large eggs
1 tablespoon heavy cream
1 teaspoon kosher salt
½ teaspoon black pepper
¾ cup grated Colby Jack cheese
Chopped scallions, chopped fresh parsley and basil for garnish

While the dough is rising, heat the olive oil in a pan and add in the ground chourico, shallots and tomatoes. As the tomatoes cook they will burst open and the mixture will thicken a bit. Portuguese chourico is already smoked, so you are really cooking down the shallots and tomatoes. Once cooked, allow the mixture to cool completely.

Once the dough is ready to use, beat together the eggs, heavy cream, salt and pepper in a small bowl and set it aside.

Preheat your oven to 450 degrees F. Spray a pizza stone or baking sheet with non-stick cooking spray. Gently work the dough by pressing it slightly on your pan from the center outward to push it out to the edges. Make a ½ inch ridge around the edge of your dough so that the egg mixture will not run off. Using a spoon spread the egg mixture around. Add half of your cheese. Add the potatoes and chourico mixture and then top the pizza with the remaining cheese.

Place your pizza on the bottom rack of your oven for ten minutes and then on the top rack for a final ten minutes, or until the bottom is crispy and the top is golden brown turning if necessary. Carefully remove from oven and garnish with fresh scallions, parsley and basil. Enjoy!

Make-Your-Own-Pizza Night

Just about everyone loves pizza! So what could be more fun than inviting a few friends over for a casual and effortless pizza party? My boys sometimes chose this fun activity for a birthday party or sleepover. As a family, make a list of your favorite toppings. Some of ours include pepperoni (we prefer turkey pepperoni), green bell peppers, fresh garlic, olives, ham, assorted cheeses, onions, pesto, mushrooms, cooked crumbled bacon, barbecue chicken, and meatballs. Be sure to have any meats that need to be cooked prepared before your guests arrive. This can be done a couple of days in advance.

For a change of pace, get creative! Try topping your pizza with caramelized onions, my Chicken Tikka Masala recipe (pg. 181), blue cheese, artichoke hearts, red onions or shallots, roasted garlic, broccoli, anchovies, Smoked Gouda, or prosciutto, and simply top it with fresh herbs and/or watercress.

Begin making the pizza dough together when your guests arrive. You can serve a few easy appetizers while the dough rises. Or, if you'd prefer, you can have the pizza dough ready for everyone. You can also make both my basic pizza dough and my multigrain pizza dough.

A make-your-own breakfast pizza party the morning after a sleepover is great fun, too!

Sweet Sticks

A wonderful variation on basic pizza dough, the addition of orange and lemon zest, vanilla and a little extra granulated sugar makes the most delightful dessert breadsticks. Of course the addition of lemon glaze doesn't hurt either!

1 tablespoon dry active yeast
½ cup sugar
1 cup warm water (100 to 115 degrees)
1 tablespoon olive oil
1 teaspoon pure vanilla extract
Zest of one orange
Zest of one large or two small lemons
1½ to 2 cups unbleached all-purpose flour
½ teaspoon kosher salt

In a large mixing bowl, combine the yeast, sugar and water. Let the mixture sit for five minutes until the yeast is activated and bubbles form.

Add in the oil, vanilla and orange and lemon zests. Then add in the flour and salt. Stir the whole mixture together with a wooden spoon just until incorporated. Turn the dough onto a floured board or counter and begin kneading. Add a little flour to the dough if it begins to stick to your hands. Do not exceed 2 cups of flour for the entire recipe. A sticky (not wet) dough makes for a great pizza--or in this case breadsticks!

Once the dough is smooth, form it into a ball and place in a clean oiled bowl. Cover the bowl with a clean towel and set it aside in a draft-free place. When the dough doubles in size, place it back onto a lightly oiled counter or board. Using your hands or a rolling pin, flatten the dough into a rectangular shape about 10 x 12 inches in size. Using a pizza cutter or sharp knife, cut dough vertically into 1-inch wide strips and then in half horizontally. Place the strips on a greased baking stone or sheet. You should end up with twenty 5 x 6-inch breadsticks.

Bake the breadsticks for 15 to 20 minutes--or until they're a little golden on top and crisp on the bottom.

Make your Orange Glaze while your breadsticks are baking.

Lemon Glaze

1 cup powdered sugar
¼ teaspoon pure vanilla extract
1 teaspoon lemon juice at a time

Place powdered sugar in a small bowl and stir in vanilla extract and enough additional lemon juice--one teaspoon at a time--to get a good consistency for drizzling. Drizzle this incredible glaze very liberally over your breadsticks. Then open wide!

Note: Substitute fresh orange juice for a refreshing lemon glaze.

Notes and Memories

Family Game Nights

Sloppy Joe Sliders

Sausage and Pepper Heros

The Great BLT with a Kick

Oatmeal Chocolate Chip Cream Cheese Bars

Chocolate Peanut Butter Oat Bars

Orange Vanilla Sugar Cookies

For me, the sounds of a timer ticking away, the clattering of dice across a board, and bursts of friendly laughter always bring back years of memories. You might wonder--with all of the flashy technology these days, aren't board games a thing of the past? I think not! When my boys return home from college for holiday breaks or weekends, you'd better believe board games of all kinds come out!

Passing the time by watching television or playing one-player games is easy. However, planning a family game night takes some doing, as families are busy and pulled in a thousand different directions every day. But if you put in the effort, the payoff is well worth it. Just like a quiet, scheduled family dinner, regular family game nights teach children to follow rules, communicate, cooperate and share. They give the whole family an opportunity to enjoy interacting with one another. And they build lasting memories.

Board games also give you a big bang for your buck! They're easily found at great prices at thrift stores, used book stores or online. You can even try swapping out your games with another family for a month or so for a cost-free change of pace.

Best of all, parents who play games with their children provide them with more than entertainment—they give them a special hour of undivided attention, a place to belong and a sense of identity. **There's power in an hour!**

One of the best parts of a family board game night is creating a delicious menu of fun foods to share. If the game doesn't keep your family around the table, these snacks certainly will! Whether you're playing cards, Scrabble, Monopoly, or Bananagrams, your hearts, minds and tummies will be well satisfied!

Sloppy Joe Sliders

1 pound 93 % lean ground turkey or beef
2 garlic cloves, minced
½ red onion, minced
½ green bell pepper, diced
½ teaspoon kosher salt
¼ teaspoon ground pepper
¼ cup chili sauce or ketchup
2 tablespoons molasses
1 teaspoon yellow mustard or ½ teaspoon ground mustard
1 tablespoon white distilled vinegar
Tiny rolls for sliders

In a sauté pan, cook the meat, garlic, onion, bell pepper, salt and pepper together until the meat is thoroughly browned--about 5 to 6 minutes. Move the meat to the sides of the pan. Add the ketchup, molasses, ground mustard and vinegar to the center of your pan. These ingredients will make up your sauce, which will have the perfect balance of sweetness, tartness and spice. Heat the sauce for two minutes. Stir in the meat, coating it completely with your super-sloppy, delicious sauce. Serve on tiny slider rolls for maximum fun.

Sausage and Pepper Heros

Feeds a Crowd

½ cup olive oil
2 pounds sweet Italian sausage, spicy sausage or your favorite Italian turkey sausage
3 red bell peppers, sliced
3 green bell peppers, sliced
3 large onions, sliced
1 (6-ounce) can tomato paste
1 cup Marsala, Port or other favorite sweet red wine
1 (14.5-ounce) can diced tomatoes
6 garlic cloves, minced
2 teaspoons kosher salt
1 tablespoon dried oregano
1 tablespoon dried basil
1 teaspoon dried thyme
1 tablespoon fresh red crushed pepper (Pimento Moida) or 1/2 teaspoon red crushed pepper flakes
10 to 12 fresh hoagie rolls

Heat the oil in a large skillet. Brown your sausages on all sides and remove from pan. Add in your peppers, onions and garlic. Sauté the vegetables until they're almost tender, then add in the tomato paste, wine, diced tomatoes, garlic, salt, oregano, basil, thyme and red crushed pepper. Cook the sauce for about five minutes. Cut sausage links into ½-inch slices and add back into the pan. Reduce the heat and let the sausages simmer for about 20 to 30 minutes, stirring occasionally. Serve with your favorite rolls.

The Great BLT with a Kick

Makes 4 hearty sandwiches or wraps

There are several things to consider when making a good ol' BLT. I admit that I do not take the construction of my BLT lightly!

Bacon, lettuce and tomato sandwiches have a long history in America. These crispy, savory, smoky sandwiches transcend demographics, religions and regions, and have been enjoyed in many variations by most American families for decades.

Building both texture and intense flavor is the key to creating a truly great BLT sandwich. When it comes to bread, use the type you like best. I enjoy a hearty, thick bread with my BLT because it can stand up to the amount of bacon, lettuce, tomato and mayonnaise I like to put on it. The thickness of your bacon will depend on your personal preference. If you like crispy bacon, try using thin-sliced or regular bacon, which crisps up nicely. If you prefer your bacon more tender, thicker slices would be your best bet. If you don't eat pork, turkey bacon makes a delicious substitute. How you eat your bacon is up to you. All I know is that there's nothing worse than a BLT with too little bacon. The more bacon the better – **so pile it on!**

Now, when it comes to tomatoes, I like to use hearty beefsteak varieties, as they have fewer seeds, a sweeter, firmer, more delicious flesh, and less water. No one likes a soggy sandwich! Heirloom tomatoes, with their variety of colors and flavors, make a great summertime choice.

Believe it or not, your choice of lettuce really matters. Romaine tends to be bitter, but Bibb, red and green leaf lettuces are sweet and have a nice soft texture. While iceberg lettuce is typically used on BLTs, I find it almost flavorless--not to mention that it's mostly water and has little nutritional value compared to other greens. Arugula is a great choice because of its interesting texture and peppery flavor.

Last but not least—the mayo! With a little imagination, your mayo can be your sandwich's best flavor enhancer. That's why I love my recipe for Chipotle Mayonnaise! If you aren't a fan of heat, try adding a little lemon or lime juice and grated garlic to your mayo instead.

Chipotle Mayonnaise

½ cup mayonnaise
1 chipotle chili in adobo sauce
1 teaspoon adobo sauce from chipotle peppers
1 garlic clove, grated (I love using my microplane for this task)
1 tablespoon chopped cilantro
1 teaspoon lemon juice

Combine all of the ingredients in a blender and set aside in your refrigerator until you're ready to use them. You can make this recipe a couple of days in advance if need be.

BLT

1 pound bacon, cooked up crispy
1 large beefsteak, vine-ripened or heirloom tomato, sliced
1 head Bibb lettuce, bunch of arugula or red or green leaf lettuce
1 ripe avocado
½ teaspoon fresh lemon juice
A sprinkle of Slap Ya Mama seasoning or a little salt, pepper and garlic powder
Your favorite bread, toasted (the thicker the bread the better)

Mash your avocado with lemon juice and a little Slap Ya Mama seasoning. Lay out the toasted bread slices and spread one side of each slice with Chipotle Mayonnaise. Spread the other slice of bread with the avocado mixture. Place ¼ of your bacon, 2 lettuce leaves (or a handful of arugula) and 2 slices of tomato on top of the avocado. Close the sandwich with the remaining slices of bread. Press downward slightly before slicing each sandwich in half with a serrated knife.

Variations: Try making a salad or topping a baked potato with BLT ingredients. Or add bacon and chipotle mayonnaise to your potato salad. You can also substitute your favorite multigrain wrap for the bread.

Oatmeal Chocolate Chip Cream Cheese Bars

My mom once made a chocolate chip cream cheese bar recipe that almost knocked my socks off into the dryer! She used refrigerated cookie dough for her bars. They were incredible, and I couldn't stop eating them. Here's my version of her recipe.

Cookie Dough

1 cup salted butter, softened
2 cups unbleached all-purpose flour
1 cup granulated sugar
1 cup light brown sugar
2 large eggs
1 tablespoon pure vanilla extract
2 ½ cups rolled or old-fashioned oats
1 ½ cups high quality chopped milk chocolate or milk chocolate chips
1 teaspoon baking powder
1 teaspoon baking soda
½ teaspoon kosher salt

Filling

2 (8-ounce) packages cream cheese, softened
2 large eggs
1 tablespoon pure vanilla extract
1 teaspoon pure almond extract
½ cup granulated sugar

Pulse the oats in a food processor for a few seconds. In a large mixing bowl, cream the butter and both sugars together until they're light and fluffy. Add in the eggs and the vanilla extract. Mix up well.

In another bowl, combine oats, flour, baking powder, soda and salt. Add this dry mixture into your wet mixture and mix them together until a soft dough forms. Fold in the chocolate pieces. Then, form the dough into a log and wrap it in waxed paper. Refrigerate the dough until you're ready to use it.

For the filling, thoroughly mix together the cream cheese, eggs, extracts and granulated sugar.

Spray the bottom of a 9 x 13-inch baking pan with non-stick butter spray. Unwrap your cookie dough and cut it into 1-inch slices.

Place one layer of dough pieces on the bottom of the baking pan. Spread your filling over the dough. Place the rest of the cookie dough pieces on top. Bake in a 350 degree oven for 45 minutes. Cool, cut into 2-inch squares and enjoy!

Chocolate Peanut Butter Oat Bars

My good old friend Tracey, who lived nearby when my boys were young, loved a lot of the same things I did. We loved homeschooling, the great outdoors and sweets! We always found it amusing that many of our field trips and unit studies revolved around food. Tracey was tall and thin and resembled the beautiful Jodi Foster, but I never held it against her! Tracey and I would often share recipes, talk about food, imagine food and of course we ATE food together all of the time.

During the morning hours of February 25, 2000 our family experienced a devastating house fire. Fortunately, everyone, with the exception of our two precious cats, Lucky and Tabitha, escaped the flames. I also lost all of my recipes. After the fire, Tracey, along with many other friends and family, wrote down all of the recipes I had shared with them, as well as those they had once passed onto me. I often remind folks to share their recipes with others.

Tracey and I particularly loved eating these Chocolate Peanut Butter Bars. We always ate them with a cup of tea. I think of her every time I make them.

Bars

1 cup old-fashioned rolled oats
1 cup boiling water
½ cup salted butter, softened
½ cup raw honey
1 large egg
1 cup unbleached all-purpose flour
½ teaspoon baking soda
½ cup smooth or chunky peanut butter
1 tablespoon pure vanilla extract

Frosting

1/3 cup creamy peanut butter
2 to 3 tablespoons of milk
1 cup semi-sweet chocolate chips (you can also use carob chips)

Here's a tip for you: Use the butter wrapper to grease a 9 x 13-inch baking pan. Preheat your oven to 350 degrees F.

Soak your oats in boiling water. In a bowl, cream together the butter, honey, egg, peanut butter and vanilla extract. Add the soaked oats to the mix and stir. Stir in the flour and baking soda.

Spread the mixture in the prepared baking pan. Bake for 10 to 15 minutes. Let it cool.

While the mixture cools, heat up your milk. Add in the peanut butter and chocolate chips and stir until everything melts together.

Once the bars have cooled a bit, spread the chocolate frosting over top and refrigerate or freeze until completely cold. Once they're chilled, cut them into bars.

Our family enjoys these best when they are nice and cold. I still love them with a good cup of tea…they'd be even better if Tracey were here!

Orange Vanilla Sugar Cookies

Here is a no-fail sugar cookie recipe that anyone can make anytime. The butter is melted so that it easily mixes into the recipe. A little vegetable oil keeps the cookies chewy without affecting their flavor, and the cream cheese keeps them tender and gives them a delicious creamy tartness. I like to double the recipe and freeze some to give away!

The final dough will be slightly softer than most cookie doughs. For best results, handle the dough as briefly and gently as possible when shaping your cookies. Overworking the dough will result in flatter, denser cookies.

Makes 2 dozen cookies

2 ½ cups unbleached all-purpose flour
½ teaspoon baking soda
1 teaspoon aluminum-free baking powder
1 ½ cups granulated sugar
2 ounces cream cheese, cut into 8 pieces
6 tablespoons salted butter, melted and still warm
1/3 cup vegetable oil
1 large egg
1 tablespoon milk
1 tablespoon pure vanilla extract
Zest of two large oranges
½ cup raw sugar for rolling

Preheat your oven to 350 degrees F. Place one rack in the middle of the oven. Spray a baking stone or sheet with non-stick cooking spray.

In a medium-sized bowl, whisk together the flour, baking soda and baking powder. Set the mixture aside.

Place the granulated sugar, cream cheese and warm melted butter in a mixing bowl. Whisk them to combine.

Add in the vegetable oil and stir until it's incorporated.

Add in the egg, milk, vanilla and orange zest, and continue to whisk them until they're smooth. Add in the flour mixture and mix until a soft dough forms.

Divide the dough into 24 equal pieces, which should equal about 2 tablespoons each.

Use your best kitchen tool (your hands) to roll the dough into balls. Working in batches, roll the balls in raw sugar to coat them and place them in evenly-spaced rows on a prepared baking sheet. Use the bottom of a drinking glass to flatten the dough into circles about 2 inches in diameter.

Bake the cookies, one batch at a time, in the center rack of the oven for 12 to 14 minutes or until the edges are set and just beginning to brown. Rotate the tray after 7 minutes of baking. Once the cookies come out of the oven, resist touching them (if you can) and let them cool on the baking sheet for 5 minutes. Using a wide spatula, transfer these beauties onto a wire rack and allow them to cool completely. Now you can enjoy! Crisp on the outside and chewy on the inside…you just made the perfect sugar cookie!

COOKIE BAKING TIPS

1. Are your cookies coming out hard and dry? Try substituting half of the granulated sugar in your recipe with brown sugar. Unlike regular sugar, brown sugar contains both glucose and fructose, which pulls moisture from the air, even after the cookies have been baked. The result is cookies that are not only moist and chewy, but deeper in color and flavor.

2. Take your cookies out of the oven before they are finished baking all the way. They should be just a touch undercooked. Cookies continue to harden once they are removed from the oven.

3. We unfortunately never have trouble keeping our cookies fresh because we eat them way too quickly, but if you do manage to store your cookies, place them in a container or freezer bag with a piece of sliced bread to keep them fresh! Change the bread slice every couple of days.

4. Always preheat your oven before baking your cookies unless otherwise stated.

Under The Stars

AROUND THE CAMPFIRE

Hot Cocoa with Peppermint Whipped Cream

Maple Wheat Cloverleaf Rolls

Spread the Love Spiced Carrot Marmalade

Warm and Toasty Minestrone Soup

Double Peanut Butter Chocolate S'mores

A HIKE IN THE WOODS

Southern Sweet Tea with a Twist

Trail Mix

Granola Clusters

I have always loved spending time with my family in the evenings. There's something so soothing and alluring about nighttime; as soon as the sun goes down our bodies seem to know it's time to relax and reflect. As far back as I can remember I have always loved putting my pajamas on early during the winter months.

As a little girl, my father would often invite me to come outside on cold, clear winter nights and look at the stars with him. What little girl doesn't adore her daddy?

Off I went—cozily bundled up--to catch a glimpse of the universe through his perfectly positioned telescope. In my eyes, my dad could do anything – even help me touch the moon!

My sons have always shared my and my father's love of the stars. When my boys were young, we spent a lot of time stargazing in warmer months. But we also found a way to enjoy the wonders of the heavens year round, in any weather. We had a little home planetarium that, once lit, beautifully displayed the stars and planets. We spent many evenings in the stillness of their room, gazing upward, talking, reflecting and laughing together. Laser pointer in hand, we marveled at the celestial world that, for all its enormity, fit perfectly on their bedroom ceiling.

My boys still enjoy looking at the stars. Nowadays, it is they who invite my husband and I to discover the wonders they find.

In spring and summer months our family often enjoyed an evening walk. In the dark and peaceful stillness of the night, every sight and sound seemed more intense and more exhilarating. With great delight, we watched the wind move through the moonlit trees and listened for the rustling of small creatures through the brush. We especially loved to hear the call of the barred owl as it called out "Who cooks for you? Who cooks for you?"

When they were children, our boys spent many summer evenings catching fireflies. The tiny creatures hovered by the hundreds in the twilight air, winking and twinkling and begging to be captured. Vavo (my mother), who loved both fireflies and evening adventures, would often accompany us on our quest. We would come inside the house, glass jars in hand, to show off our little glowing treasures. Then back outside we'd go to let our new friends fly again under the glow of the moon.

Some of our favorite evening memories are from when we lived on Biltmore Lake in Asheville, North Carolina. Biltmore Lake is a 62-acre lake surrounded on three sides by majestic mountains. On chilly fall nights, we loved nothing more than to sit huddled around the warmth of the community campfire pit, listening to animal sounds, talking and singing campfire songs like "I Am My Own Grandpa." At dusk we would watch the shadows of mountains creep across the face of the lake. At night, we would gaze upward at the towering black shapes the mountains made against the dark purple sky. Our little group seemed so small against those mountains!

What could be better than a night with family by the campfire? Well, how about a fireside meal made up of Maple Wheat Cloverleaf Rolls with Spiced Carrot Marmalade, a hot cup of minestrone soup, and Double Peanut Chocolate S'mores? Now that's a meal that's sure to create a memory that will last a lifetime! A tip—topping this meal off with a cup of steaming hot chocolate adorned with a fresh dollop of homemade Peppermint Whipped Cream will really hit the spot, especially on very chilly nights!

AROUND THE CAMPFIRE

Hot Cocoa with Peppermint Whipped Cream

Your favorite hot chocolate
1 pint of heavy whipping cream
1 teaspoon pure vanilla extract
1 bag of red and white peppermint star candies

Using a food processor, chop a few of the candies until they're roughly crushed, and chop the rest into a fine powder. In a mixing bowl, beat the heavy whipping cream and vanilla until it's thick. Fold in your crushed candies. Make hot chocolate and place a big dollop of cream on top. Enjoy!

TIP: If you don't have a food processor, you can release your frustrations by placing the candies in a plastic bag, sealing it, and crushing them with a rolling pin or mallet. However, if you do use a food processor, you end up with a fine peppermint sugar, along with a few nice chunks of candy for texture. Go buy yourself a food processor! You deserve it!

Maple Wheat Cloverleaf Rolls

1 tablespoon dry active yeast
1 cup warm water (100 to 110 degrees F)
1½ cups unbleached bread flour, plus more for kneading
1 cup whole wheat flour
3 tablespoons pure maple syrup or raw honey
2 tablespoons butter, melted
1 teaspoon kosher salt
Non-stick cooking spray
1 tablespoon water
1 large egg

Dissolve the yeast in 1 cup of warm water and let it stand for 5 minutes to proof. Don't you just love the smell of yeast proofing?

In a large mixing bowl combine unbleached bread flour, whole wheat flour and salt.

Add the yeast mixture, maple syrup or honey and melted butter to your dry mixture and stir it just until blended.

Turn the dough out onto a floured surface.

Knead the dough until it's smooth and elastic (about 8 minutes) adding enough flour--1 tablespoon at a time--to prevent it from sticking to your hands (the dough should feel sticky, but not too sticky).

Wash your bowl in warm water and dry it well. Spray the bowl with non-stick cooking spray and place the dough back in. Cover it with a cloth and keep in a dry, draft-free place until it doubles in size. Once you think the dough has doubled, press two fingers into it. If an indentation remains, the dough has risen enough. Punch the dough down, cover it, and let it rest for 5 minutes.

Preheat your oven to 425 degrees F. Coat 12 muffin cups with cooking spray. Divide the dough into 12 equal portions. Divide each of the portions into 3 pieces and shape each piece into a ball. Place 3 balls in each muffin cup. Once baked, this bread will have such a pretty cloverleaf shape!

Cover the muffin tin with a dish towel and let your dough rise for 35 minutes or until it has doubled in size. Uncover the dough. Combine your egg with 1 tablespoon of water and brush the mixture over the rolls.

Bake the rolls at 425 degrees F for 12 minutes or until they're lightly browned. Serve them warm with Spiced Carrot Marmalade.

Spread the Love Spiced Carrot Marmalade

The luminous amber color of this marmalade will make your mouth water before your lips even touch its sweet and spicy goodness. I have always enjoyed developing recipes that can be shared with others, and over the years our family has created many edible gifts. Recently, we filled pretty mason jars with this delicious marmalade and gave it as gifts to family and friends. A bit of raffia attached to a rustic-looking tag added the perfect touch to a beautiful present we were happy to share with our friends.

Just as one of the verses of a song from my all-time favorite movie "The Sound of Music" declares: "A bell's not a bell 'til you ring it/ A song's not a song 'til you sing it/ Love in your heart wasn't put there to stay/ Love isn't love 'til you give it away!" Spread some love by making this for someone special, and by all means enjoy it with your family!

Makes 4 cups

2 pounds grated carrots
4 cups granulated sugar
1 teaspoon each ground cinnamon, ground nutmeg, and ground ginger
½ teaspoon each ground allspice, ground mace and ground cloves
Zest and juice of one lemon
Zest and juice of two oranges

Place the grated carrots in a heavy saucepan and cover them with water. Simmer the carrots over medium-high heat for 20 minutes, or until they're tender. Drain off the excess water.

While your carrots are simmering away, measure your sugar, cinnamon, nutmeg, ginger, allspice, mace, and cloves into a large bowl.

While you wait for your carrots to soften, sterilize your canning jars and lids. This prevents harmful bacteria from growing in your marmalade and allows you to store it for a longer time. To sterilize your equipment, place your jars and lids into a deep pan filled halfway with water. Bring the water to a boil for about 5 minutes. Turn off the heat and allow the jars to sit for a couple of minutes. Then, using tongs, carefully place the jars and lids onto a plate to cool.

Drain the carrots well. Return them to the saucepan and add in the sugar and spices.

Add the orange and lemon zest and juice to the carrot mixture. Slowly stir the mixture until it is completely blended.

Simmer the mixture over low heat, stirring frequently for 45 minutes, or until it's thick and glossy.

Spoon the marmalade into the sterilized jars, carefully wiping off any excess that spills onto the outside of the jars. Run a damp paper towel along the inside lip of the jar so that it stays nice and clean. Allow the marmalade to cool. Once cooled, place the lid on and close it tightly. You can store your marmalade in the refrigerator for up to 30 days.

"Love in your heart wasn't put there to stay/ Love isn't love 'til you give it away!" – The Sound of Music

Warm and Hearty Minestrone Soup

There's nothing better than sitting around a campfire on a cold evening with a delicious mug of hot soup warming up your hands and belly!

1 pound lean ground turkey
1 onion, diced
4 celery ribs, diced
2 cloves garlic, minced
2 tablespoons canola or olive oil
2 teaspoons Italian seasoning
1 teaspoon dried thyme
2 tablespoons garlic powder
2 tablespoons onion powder
1 tablespoon fresh red crushed pepper or ½ teaspoon dried red pepper flakes
2 (14.5-ounce) cans diced tomatoes (you will use the juice too)
3 tablespoons or so Better than Bouillon Chicken Base
1 (16-ounce) bag frozen vegetables (I typically use a mixture of peas, carrots, corn and lima beans)
1 cup of your favorite small pasta, or angel hair pasta broken up into tiny pieces
Salt and pepper to taste

In a regular size soup pan, heat your oil up for a few seconds. Add in your ground turkey, onion, celery and garlic. Stir constantly until the turkey is cooked through and the vegetables are a bit tender--about 7 to 9 minutes.

Add in the tomatoes (along with the juice), Italian seasoning, thyme, garlic, onion powder, fresh red crushed pepper or pepper flakes, and salt and pepper to taste. Cook the mixture for 5 minutes, and then add in the frozen vegetables.

Add enough water to cover the pot, and then add about three tablespoons or so of the chicken base. You may need to add less or more of the base, depending on your preference. Add in one tablespoon at a time, stirring in between, until you get a flavor you like.

Allow the soup to simmer over medium heat for 30 minutes.

Add in the pasta and allow it to simmer until it's cooked. Taste the soup to see if you need to add a little more salt or pepper.

The pasta in this soup will soak up the broth. If you don't plan to eat your soup right away, or you plan to serve leftover soup later on in the week, you may have to add a little more water or chicken stock to thin it out before it's heated and served.

Double Peanut Butter Chocolate S'mores

Whenever I smell freshly baked peanut butter cookies, I'm reminded of the time my boys built a solar oven for a homeschool science fair we once organized. Nathaniel (who was seven at the time) and I (who will not admit my age) helped my then four-year-old son Alexander build the oven, and we baked the cookies together.

As a family who loves our campfires and our s'mores, we always have the quintessential graham crackers, chocolate bars and marshmallows handy. However, we do like to invent fun new ways to make these classics. Once, when I was trying to come up with a new s'more recipe, I thought of those peanut butter cookies. Then I thought, why not go all out and add peanut butter cups as well? Turns out, these s'mores were a big hit! I hope your family enjoys them as much as we do.

½ cup salted butter, softened
½ cup creamy or chunky peanut butter (I prefer using a not-so-sweet peanut butter variety)
½ cup granulated sugar
½ cup light brown sugar
½ teaspoon baking soda
½ teaspoon baking powder
1 large egg
1 tablespoon pure vanilla extract
1¼ cups unbleached all-purpose flour
Raw sugar for rolling
Peanut Butter Cups
Marshmallows

In a large mixer or bowl, cream the butter and peanut butter for just a minute. Add in the granulated sugar, brown sugar, baking soda and baking powder and mix them just until they're combined. Beat in the egg and vanilla extract. Then beat in the flour. Cover the dough and chill it for thirty minutes. Chilling the dough makes it so much easier to work with and shape.

Preheat your oven to 375 degrees F. Shape the dough into one-inch balls (be sure to make all of your cookies the same size so that they cook evenly). Roll each ball in raw sugar. The raw sugar glistens so prettily as the cookies bake!

Place the cookies two inches apart on an ungreased baking stone or cookie sheet. Press the top of each cookie with a fork, making a crisscross pattern. Bake the cookies for 8 minutes or until lightly browned. Remember to take your cookies out before they are completely cooked through because they will continue to harden as they cool. Allow them to cool completely. I know it's very hard to do, but it's worth it!

Using a stick or a metal fork with a handle, heat a marshmallow over the fire. Place it on top of a peanut butter cookie. Place a peanut butter cup on top of the marshmallow, then close the whole thing with another cookie. Yes, these are just as good as they sound!

A HIKE IN THE WOODS

An evening hike in the woods is so much more fun if you take along these refreshments!

Southern Sweet Tea with a Twist

4 quarts of filtered water
2 large family-sized black pekoe tea bags
2 spiced chai tea bags
1 cup granulated sugar
1 cup filtered water

First, bring the water, black pekoe tea bags and spiced Chai tea bags to a boil in a large Dutch oven. Once the water is boiling, cover the pot and allow the tea to steep for about ten minutes, or until it reaches the strength you prefer.

While the tea steeps, create your simple syrup. Bring 1cup of water and 1cup of granulated sugar to a boil, carefully stirring for about five minutes--or until the sugar dissolves and you achieve a thick, syrupy consistency.

Remove the tea bags from the water and carefully stir in your simple syrup. Allow the tea to cool before refrigerating it.

Trail Mix

Easy to make and light to carry, this trail mix will give you the energy needed to keep walking 'til morning!

2 cups honey-roasted peanuts
1 cup whole pecans
1 cup sunflower kernels
1 cup dark raisins
1 cup light raisins

Combine all of the ingredients in a bowl, store in a plastic storage bag and prepare for the great outdoors! If you're not a fan of raisins, other types of dried fruit like mango, cranberries, pineapple, apples and banana chips may be substituted.

Granola Clusters

This recipe requires a little more effort than the trail mix, but it's the perfect snack for a long (or short) evening hike!

Homemade Granola

3 ½ cups old fashioned rolled oats
½ cup flax seeds
¼ cup pumpkin seeds
¼ cup sesame seeds
¼ cup slivered almonds
½ cup walnut pieces
¼ cup walnut oil
1 tablespoon ground cinnamon
1 teaspoon freshly ground nutmeg
¾ teaspoon kosher or sea salt
¼ cup dark brown sugar
2 tablespoons raw honey
2 tablespoons pure maple syrup
2 cups dried fruit combination (I use dried cranberries, dried Pomegranate cranberries, figs or dried fruit bit mixtures with raisins, apples, apricots, etc.)
1 egg white

Preheat your oven to 375 degrees F.

In a large bowl, mix all of the ingredients together, with the exception of the egg white.

In a small bowl or cup whisk the egg white until it is frothy and foamy. Stir it into the granola.

Spread your granola out in an even layer on your prepared baking sheet (this is a great job for the kiddos). Bake the granola for ten minutes.

Remove the granola from the oven and let it cool COMPLETELY. Once cooled, it should be clumpy. If you pour the granola off the baking sheet while it's still hot, it will break up into loose granola instead of clumping up properly.

When the granola is completely cool, break it up into chunks and transfer it to an airtight container for storage.

Notes and Memories

PLAYING WITH YOUR FOOD

PASTA DISHES

Caesar's Tableside Salad

Homemade Fettuccini with Bolognese Sauce

Roasted Vegetable Lasagna

Spaghetti with Spicy Sausage and Pepper Sauce

Sausage Ravioli with Brown Butter Sauce

Lavender Almond Panna Cotta with Roasted Cherries

How surprised I was when I opened my Christmas gift from our dear friends, the Forsters. Having never made homemade pasta before, I was delighted to open my gift to see my first shiny pasta maker looking up at me! Two days later our family was in the kitchen making our first batch of homemade fettuccini with our new pasta maker. We made the beautiful yellow dough by simply mixing unbleached all-purpose flour, eggs, oil, a bit of salt and a little water together. Once the dough was incorporated, we all took turns kneading **the heck out of it**! Knead, knead, knead… and then … knead some more!

A few days later (New Year's Eve actually) the Forsters joined us for an evening of mixing, kneading, rolling and eating! We all had way too much fun making dinner together.

We adorned our homemade fettuccini with my rich and hearty bolognese sauce. Fresh pasta absorbs sauces very well, and boy, is this sauce terrific.

I can hardly wait for you to make this with your family and friends. We all had so much fun, and we certainly earned our dinner that night! Everyone was casually dressed, and it's a good thing, because by the time we sat down to enjoy our homemade pasta and sauce, we all laughed as we realized that many of us were wearing flour on our clothing, and on our shoes and some of us even had flour on our faces – I'll never say who! To think that we could have gone out to eat or simply opened a box of dried pasta, but instead we created a memory that will last a lifetime.

Making homemade pasta isn't always possible, but these recipes are fantastic with store-bought fresh or good-quality dried pastas. Making homemade pasta once in a while is just another way to create an eventful family meal.

Caesar's Tableside Salad

Serves 4

Many people assume that the traditional Caesar salad is named after the famed Roman emperor, but in fact it is named for Caesar Cardini, an Italian chef working in Tijuana, Mexico in the 1920s. You may recognize the Cardini name on salad dressings in your grocery store. Caesar was well-known for the dramatic way he served his salad tableside at his restaurant. It is said that Julia Child enjoyed Caesar's salad at his restaurant as a child, and that Cardini himself served it to her family. I love this salad because the dressing and croutons can be made ahead of time.

½ cup good quality extra virgin olive oil, plus a little extra for croutons
3 cloves fresh garlic, peeled, smashed, then minced
½ teaspoon freshly ground salt
½ teaspoon finely ground black pepper
1 day-old baguette, cut into bite size pieces (we love chunks)
½ teaspoon dried thyme
1 teaspoon anchovy paste or ½ teaspoon of Worcestershire sauce
2 large eggs
1/3 cup lemon juice
¾ cup freshly grated Parmesan cheese
3 large or 5 small heads of romaine lettuce, rinsed, dried and torn – discard outer leaves if necessary

In a bowl, whisk together the olive oil, garlic, salt, and pepper in a bowl. Set aside for half an hour or more.

Place the bread cubes in a mixing bowl. Toss them in a little olive oil or melted butter and thyme, then place them on a baking sheet or broiler pan. Use a sheet or pan with high edges to ensure the oil doesn't leak out onto the bottom of the oven and leave a smoky mess. (This is a tip I learned from experience!). I actually prefer to use my broiler pan, because the dark color of the pan results in very crispy croutons.

Broil the croutons for a couple of minutes until lightly browned. Croutons burn rapidly so please be attentive. (I learned that from experience, too!)

Once your croutons are out of the oven, begin making the dressing. Add the anchovy paste and eggs to the garlic oil mixture and whisk them together until they're very creamy. Stir in the lemon juice and half of the Parmesan cheese.

When ready to serve, place the lettuce in a chilled salad bowl, pour dressing over it and toss. Add in the croutons and the remaining Parmesan cheese.

Homemade Fettuccini with Bolognese Sauce

Feeds 6 to 8 hungry people

Pasta Dough

4 cups unbleached all-purpose flour
4 large eggs, plus one egg yolk
¼ cup extra virgin olive oil
1 teaspoon kosher salt
A little water or heavy cream

Bolognese Sauce

6 strips of bacon, cut into small pieces
1 ¾ pounds 93 % ground beef
1 large onion, chopped
1 green bell pepper, chopped
1 cup finely grated carrots
1 cup finely chopped celery
5 cloves garlic, minced
1 ½ cups dry white wine
1 cup low-sodium chicken broth
28 ounces crushed tomatoes
6 ounces tomato paste
2 teaspoons each dried thyme, basil and oregano
2 teaspoons kosher salt or to taste
1 tablespoon Pimento Moida or fresh red crushed pepper or ½ teaspoon dried red pepper flakes (less if you do not like spicy)
1 cup heavy cream

For the sauce, place the bacon in a large pot over medium heat and sauté until brown and crispy. Add the ground beef, breaking it up with a spoon, until browned--about 8 to 10 minutes.

Add in the onions, green peppers, carrots, celery, and garlic. Cook the mixture for 10 minutes more, or until softened.

Add in the wine and allow the sauce to cook for about five minutes. Add the chicken stock, crushed tomatoes, tomato paste, thyme, basil, oregano, salt, pepper. Simmer the sauce for two hours on low. Finish the sauce off with the heavy cream. As always, taste the sauce and adjust the seasonings to your liking.

Homemade Pasta

To make homemade pasta, combine eggs, egg yolk, oil and salt in a small bowl. Place flour on the counter and make a deep well. Pour wet ingredients inside the well and using a fork, begin to combine the flour and the egg mixture until a dough forms. No need to worry if the wet mixture escapes the flour. Just get a little dirty and use your hands to mix and reign it back in.

Add a little water or cream if dough is a little dry. Knead the dough heavily until it forms a smooth ball. The more dough you have, the harder it is to knead, and the longer it will take. If you are cooking for a large group, you may want to knead in batches. It's also fun for everyone to help!

Once the dough is smooth, cut it into smaller pieces. Begin on the highest number of your pasta maker. After your first pass, fold the dough in half. (Fold in half only once.) Work your way down one number each time you pass the dough through. Dusting the pasta dough with flour after a couple of passes will help it to not stick. Keep passing your dough through the pasta maker until it's rolled out to your desired thickness. Use your pasta maker to cut into fettuccini. Place the dough in small batches into salted boiling water. Fresh pasta only takes about two minutes to cook.

Serve al dente with Bolognese Sauce and enjoy!

MAINTAINING YOUR PASTA MAKER IS EASY

1. To prevent steel parts and wires from rusting, keep your pasta maker away from water.

2. Wipe off any flour with a pastry brush.

3. Use a plastic scraper to remove any sticking dough.

4. Lubricate your machine from time to time. For most mechanical pasta makers, you can place a drop of mineral oil where each roller meets the body.

5. Store your pasta maker in its original box in a dry place.

6. If repairs are ever needed, I would not suggest taking your pasta maker apart. It is very difficult to put back together.

Roasted Vegetable Lasagna

Serves a crowd

Filled with layers of flavorful roasted vegetables and a thick and creamy béchamel sauce, even the most discriminating meat lover will fall in love with this lasagna.

Roasted Vegetables

1 head broccoli, separated into florets
1 head cauliflower, separated into florets
1 bunch of asparagus, ends removed
3 to 4 carrots, peeled and chopped
2 sweet onions, peeled and chopped
A large bunch of fresh spinach leaves
2 tablespoons or so olive oil
1 teaspoon kosher salt

Béchamel Sauce

7 tablespoons salted butter
7 tablespoons unbleached all-purpose flour
4 cups milk
1 teaspoon kosher salt
1 teaspoon Creole seasoning
½ teaspoon freshly ground nutmeg
1 cup freshly grated Parmesan cheese
Non-stick spray for 9 x 13-inch baking dish

1 pound cooked lasagna noodles

Preheat your oven to 400 degrees F.

Separate your vegetables and arrange them into columns in your roasting pan (I actually like to use the bottom of my broiler pan). Drizzle them with olive oil and sprinkle them with salt.

I never mix my vegetables together, because each vegetable cooks at a different rate. Separating the veggies allows me to take each of them out when they have completed cooking..

Place the veggies in the oven. The asparagus and onion will be ready after just five minutes, and will be the first to come out of the oven. The broccoli and cauliflower will take about ten minutes, and the carrots will take 15 minutes. The natural sugar in the carrots will add a lovely flavor to your lasagna!

Be sure to stir or turn over the vegetables half way through the roasting process. Do not overcook your vegetables. Roasted vegetables should be prepared like pasta - they should always have a little bite to them.

Your vegetables will also continue to cook in the lasagna in the oven, so take them out a bit before they are fully cooked. Chop the broccoli, cauliflower and asparagus so it will be uniform with your carrots and onions.

Set the cooked vegetables aside while you make the Béchamel sauce.

To make the Béchamel sauce, melt your butter in a medium saucepan over low heat. Add in the flour and stir until the mixture is smooth. Gradually whisk in the milk until it's smooth and creamy. The mixture will begin to bubble. To prevent scorching your sauce, keep the heat low. Once the Béchamel has thickened, remove it from the stove and add your salt, Creole seasoning and nutmeg.

Spray a 9 x 13-inch baking pan with a non-stick cooking spray. Place some of the roasted vegetables on the bottom. Spread a layer of spinach leaves. Place a layer of lasagna noodles over top. Spread your Béchamel sauce over the top of your noodles. Sprinkle some of the Parmesan over top. Continue adding vegetables, spinach leaves, noodles, sauce and cheese until all of your ingredients are used. End with a nice layer of Béchamel and sprinkle freshly grated Parmesan cheese on top.

Cover and bake in a 350 degree F oven for 40 minutes. Remove the cover and set the lasagna back in the oven for an additional 10 minutes. This will allow it to brown up a bit. Enjoy this hearty meal with a nice salad.

PASTA TIPS

1. Choose a good quality pasta – it makes an immense difference in flavor
2. Do not overcrowd your pasta when cooking - choose the right size pot
3. Make sure you have enough water in your pot
4. Always cook your pasta in lightly salted water
5. Avoid sticking by placing your pasta in a boiling pot of water–pay attention and give it an occasional stir
6. Pasta should always be cooked "al-dente" which means firm, but not hard. This is especially true when noodles will be baked in the oven
7. I never add oil to my water because the sauce won't stick properly to my pasta
8. NEVER rinse your pasta – you will wash away that wonderful starchy flavor
9. Use a little of the pasta water in your sauces to thin out and to add flavor
10. Always allow lasagnas to set up before cutting into them

Spaghetti with Spicy Sausage and Pepper Sauce

My grandmother's recipe, the one I enjoyed most as a child, is now being placed in your hands. My grandmother loved to cook, and I am certain that she would be delighted to know that her sauce will be enjoyed by so many.

3 tablespoons extra-virgin olive oil
1 pound sweet or spicy Italian sausage, either ground or removed from casing and crumbled
½ green bell pepper, chopped or sliced
1 yellow onion, peeled, halved and sliced
4 cloves of garlic, minced
½ cup good red or white wine
1 (28-ounce can) crushed tomatoes
1 (14.5-ounce can) stewed tomatoes
1 (6-ounce can) tomato paste
2 bay leaves, dried or fresh
½ teaspoon dried red pepper flakes or 1 tablespoon fresh Pimento Moida
Garlic and onion powder *(My grandmother would always dust the top of the sauce with it; in another words – she put lots)*
2 teaspoons kosher salt
1 tablespoon Italian seasonings
A pinch of sugar to round out the flavors

In a very large skillet or Dutch oven, sauté the sausage until browned, but not cooked all the way through. Once you place the sausage back into the sauce, it will add flavor as it continues to cook. Transfer the browned sausage onto a plate.

Sauté the onions and green pepper in olive oil until softened--about five minutes. Add in the garlic and cook the vegetables for a minute more. Add in wine to deglaze the bottom of the pan – that is where all of the flavor is! Cook the mixture for about two minutes. Add in the remaining ingredients, including your browned sausage and let them simmer together for at least one hour.

Bring a pot of salted water to a boil. Choose your favorite pasta and cook it according to package directions--or make your own pasta! Remember that fresh pasta always cooks quicker than dried and that you ultimately want a little bite to your pasta.

Sausage Ravioli with Brown Butter Sauce

Serves two hungry people

"It was the oil in her hands…"

    Recently I visited my good friends Bill and Karlie. We were talking about my upcoming cookbook and some of the recipes and stories shared within it. We laughed, teared up, and just had a good ol' time! As we chatted about our favorite food memories, Karlie mentioned that her mom made the best cornbread stuffing that had ever touched her lips. Everyone in Karlie's family has attempted to replicate the recipe since her Momma's passing, but no one has ever been able to achieve the same flavor and texture. In Karlie's Southern accent (which I adore) she said, "*It's just never the same as Momma's; I swear, it was the oil in her hands!*"

    That same night, I made my homemade sausage ravioli with brown butter sauce. As I worked the thick, smooth pasta dough into a ball, I was reminded of Karlie's remark. I too, swear that pasta and bread just don't come out the same if I don't knead the dough by hand. Kneading dough by hand also gives me the sense that I'm part of a noble, ancient tradition. My grandmother always kneaded dough by hand and everything she made came out amazing. When I knead dough of any kind, I see her, feel her and remember . . .

Pasta Dough

2 cups unbleached all-purpose flour
2 large eggs
1 large egg yolk
½ teaspoon kosher salt
1 tablespoon olive oil
A little water

Ina small bowl beat together the eggs, egg yolk, oil and salt. Place your flour in a mound on a clean, dry surface. Make a well—a "hole" in the center of the mound--and add the mixture of eggs, egg yolk, salt, olive oil and a little water. Using a fork, beat the wet mixture inside the well and slowly incorporate all of the flour into the egg mixture. Once everything has been incorporated, it's time to have some fun!

Begin kneading the dough for about ten minutes, or until it's tight and smooth. You may need to add a tablespoon of water or so if the dough is too dry. Flour is a finicky thing!

Once the dough is tight and smooth, wrap it in plastic wrap and leave it to rest for 20 to 30 minutes. You can also keep it in the refrigerator for several days until you're ready to use! Just let the dough rest once removed from the refrigerator for 20 to 30 minutes.

While your dough rests, make your filling.

Sausage Filling

4 Italian sausages
½ sweet onion, chopped
2 cloves garlic, minced
½ teaspoon salt
¼ teaspoon allspice
½ teaspoon ground nutmeg
1 large egg

In a sauté pan, brown your sausage and onion. Add in the garlic and salt and cook two minutes more. Place mixture in a food processor and pulse until it's a bit smoother. Add in allspice and nutmeg. Allow the mixture to cool. Once the mixture is cooled, add in one egg and stir well. Reserve the pan with the sausage drippings for your brown butter sauce.

You can store your pasta and filling in the refrigerator for several days!

If you are ready to make your ravioli, cut your dough into several even pieces. Begin with one piece and cover the rest of the dough while you work. Run your first piece through your pasta machine on the thickest setting, fold it, then run it through again. Next, continue to run the dough through, decreasing the thickness each time until you're satisfied with it. Do the same with all of the other pieces.

Once your pasta dough is rolled out, place one sheet of dough on a flat surface. Starting a half-inch from the edge, place small mounds—about two tablespoons each--of sausage mixture about an inch apart in rows all the way across one of the sheets. Brush a little (not a lot) of water on the dough around each mound. This will be the glue that keeps the ravioli from opening up and keeps your filling inside. Cover the first sheet of pasta with another sheet.

Using a round cutter or a pizza cutter, cut the dough neatly between the mounds lengthwise and crosswise to create individual raviolis. Set the raviolis aside while you make your brown butter sauce.

Brown Butter Sauce

4 tablespoons salted butter
1 teaspoon dried sage or 3 fresh sage leaves
2 tablespoons heavy cream
Grind of fresh black pepper

Using a paper towel, remove some of the grease from the pan the sausage was browned in. Leave most of the bits at the bottom of the pan. Add the butter and sage to the pan and brown over medium-high heat. With a wooden spoon, scrape up all of the sausage bits on the bottom of the pan–that's how you'll add even more flavor to this sauce! Add in heavy cream (or chicken stock, if you prefer), and season with fresh black pepper.

Place the raviolis into a boiling pot of salted water. Cook them for about two to three minutes, then plate them. Top the dish with brown butter and garnish it with fresh Parmigiano Reggiano cheese. Open wide and enjoy!

Cranberry and White Chocolate Biscotti

The moment my family smells the scent of almond in the air and hears the sound of my serrated knife cutting through Biscotti, they dash into the kitchen to collect the Biscotti ends before the cookies are twice baked!

½ cup olive or vegetable oil
1 cup granulated sugar
3 large eggs
2 teaspoons pure almond extract
1 teaspoon pure vanilla extract
3¼ cups all-purpose unbleached flour
1 tablespoon aluminum-free baking powder
Zest of two oranges or lemons
¾ cup dried cranberries
½ cup white chocolate chips
½ cup pistachios, chopped, optional

Preheat your oven to 375 degrees F. In a large bowl, using a wooden spoon, mix the olive oil, sugar, eggs and both extracts together.

In a medium-sized bowl combine the flour, baking powder, orange zest, cranberries and white chocolate chips. Add the olive oil and egg mixture into the flour mixture and mix until it forms a dough. Knead a bit just until the dough comes together. Divide into two. Place the two mounds of dough on a cookie sheet and form them into wide logs. Press the logs down a little. Take care to space the logs apart, as they do expand while baking.

Bake the cookie logs for 25 minutes. Watch them carefully to ensure they don't cook all the way through. Remove them from the oven and allow them to cool. Using a serrated knife, carefully slice the logs into ½-inch pieces. Place the pieces back on the cookie sheet and bake them for an additional 6 minutes or so.

Don't forget that, like all cookies, biscotti will harden as it cools. Some folks like their biscotti drier than others. The longer they stay in, they drier they get. I always make mine crispy on the outside and a little chewy on the inside!

Tip: Dusting the cranberries and chocolate chips with a little flour before folding them into the dough will prevent them from sinking.

Lavender Almond Panna Cotta with Roasted Cherries

The Italian dessert Panna Cotta (or cooked cream) has a lovely, smooth milky consistency, and works very well with a number of different flavors. In this recipe, the marriage of almond and lavender enhance this lovely dessert. Roasting the cherries allows the natural sugars to come out, while the almonds add a nice crunch that contrasts well with the dessert's creaminess. I always encourage my family and students to consider using complementary textures when playing in the kitchen.

When using lavender--or any edible flower—please be sure to purchase culinary grade lavender. Florists, nurseries, and garden centers typically sell treated plants that are not labeled as food crops, with the exception of herbs.

I love cherries and there are several types. Rainier cherries, which are what I use in this recipe, are my favorite. You can also use Bing, Black Stone Cherries, Chelan, Choke Cherries, Lapins, Maraschinos, Morellos, Napoleons, North Stars, Spanish Cherries, Sweethearts or Tietons.

Lavender Almond Panna Cotta

Non-stick cooking spray
½ cup warm water
2 envelopes gelatin
2 cups heavy cream
2 cups half-and-half
¾ cup granulated sugar
1 ½ teaspoons pure almond extract
2 teaspoons lavender buds

Roasted Cherries

1 pound fresh cherries, pitted
4 tablespoons granulated sugar
½ teaspoon ground cinnamon
Zest of one large orange
2 tablespoons fresh orange juice
1 teaspoon lavender buds
½ cup slivered almonds, toasted

Spray 6 to 8 ramekins or small glass bowls with non-stick cooking spray and set aside.

Pour warm water into a medium-sized bowl and sprinkle gelatin over. It takes about 5 minutes for the gelatin to thicken so set aside while you work on your cream mixture.

In a heavy bottomed saucepan, heat your heavy cream, half-and-half, sugar, almond extract and lavender buds over medium heat. Stir for a few minutes--just until the sugar dissolves. Pour the mixture over the gelatin and stir until the gelatin dissolves completely.

Pour the mixture into your greased ramekins and refrigerate for at least four hours, or until the mixture has set up.

While your Panna Cotta is setting up, prepare your cherries and almonds.

Place the cherries in a baking dish. Sprinkle sugar, cinnamon, orange zest, juice and lavender buds on top. Give the mixture a quick stir to combine.

Place the cherries in a 400 degree preheated oven and roast them until they start to release their lovely juices and the sugar melts and begins to caramelize. This will take about 20 minutes. Be sure to watch the cherries very carefully because the sugar may begin to burn. (Tip: The roasted cherries can be refrigerated and then heated up on the stove top when ready to serve.)

Toast your almonds in a dry pan over medium heat, stirring constantly, until they brown a little bit. Take care not to walk away -- they will burn quickly. Set aside.

When ready to serve, run a knife around the edges of your Panna Cotta, invert it onto your serving plate and give it a little shake. (Note: Some people choose to not invert the Panna Cotta, but to rather serve it in coffee cups, wine, martini or brandy glasses, small bowls or even in a larger bowl with a pattern). I prefer inverting onto a plate. Top it with the roasted cherries and toasted almonds. Grab a spoon and enjoy!

Murder Mystery Dinners

MURDER MYSTERY DINNER MENU

Wholegrain Pan Rolls with Herbed Butter

Sour Soup

Mom's Portuguese Oven Roast

Carrot Potato Mash

Green Tomato Spice Cake with Brown Butter Icing

MEDIEVAL MURDER MYSTERY DINNER MENU

Herb Biscuits

Creamy Potato Leek Soup

Sing a Song of Six Pence French Meat Pie

Arroz Doce (Rice Pudding)

When it rains it pours…

Since the beginning of our marriage we have lived far away from our relatives, so family visits have always been very important to us.

A few years ago, while living in Asheville, North Carolina, we prepared for a visit from my parents and Peachie, a good family friend. We thought it would be great fun to host our first Murder Mystery Dinner with our special guests.

The excitement in the air was almost tangible as we prepared our celebratory Murder Mystery meal. Although the murder mystery plot was based in England, Mom and I spent the afternoon making our dinner which included two of our family's favorites -- Mom's Portuguese Style Oven Roast with Carrot Potato Mash.

Then, before our other guests arrived, all of the Murder Mystery participants went off into different rooms to change. Each had been told beforehand who they would be playing. One by one, each made his or her way downstairs in character and in costume. We all marveled at the amount of detail everyone had put into dressing in character.

Dinner was scrumptious, but it was after dinner that the real fun began. We made our way into the 1800's English Manor (or artfully decorated great room) and waited for the show to begin. Just as we were engrossing ourselves in the story, we heard the telltale grumblings of an impending storm.

Sure enough, a huge thunderstorm swept through the Blue Ridge Mountains and straight over our house. As we played out our mystery, we heard the rush of heavy rain on the rooftop. The winds picked up and the lights flickered ominously. Then, the power went out. Fortunately, we had placed lit candles everywhere to help set the murder mystery mood. I was delighted! Lighting, rain, a power outage, and the jolting, booming echo of thunder you only experience in a mountain storm . . . this was the best Murder Mystery Dinner ever!

We all sat in the glow of the candlelight, transfixed by the storm. Suddenly, the sound of cracking thunder and shattering glass made us all jump with fright. Could lightning have hit one of the front windows? We all carefully made our way to the front of the house, trembling with fear, as our favorite feline, Isabel, went running past us in the opposite direction. It turned out that Isabel, who had been sitting on top of our large armoire, had witnessed a bolt of lightning strike the tree out front. The sight of the resulting fireball had sent her leaping from the armoire in a panic, and knocking over an oil lamp in the process.

After we cleaned up the mess, everyone sat down to proceed with our mystery. Suddenly, with candle in hand, in the voice of a frightened little girl, my mom cried out, **"I don't think I want to play this anymore!"** After a quick pause, laughter erupted throughout the room! We couldn't have planned that night any better if we tried . . .

Wholegrain Pan Rolls

Who doesn't love the smell of baking bread? Your guests will be delighted as they are greeted by the scrumptious scent of these tasty, healthful multigrain rolls! This delicious whole grain recipe will leave your guests very content.

I like to bake these rolls in two 8 or 9-inch round cake pans to create a pretty wreath-like shape. I leave one wreath intact, separate the other into individual rolls, line a basket with a napkin and place the wreath and rolls within it. It makes a great centerpiece for a table.

I have also wrapped these rolls and given them away as gifts along with one of my compound butters or marmalades to enjoy. You can choose any one of the many compound butter variations listed below the recipe.

Makes 22 rolls

2 cups water
½ cup bulgur wheat
1 tablespoon dry active yeast
1 cup warm milk
½ cup rolled or old-fashioned oats
1/8 cup whole flax seeds
1/3 cup raw honey or agave syrup
2 large eggs
2 teaspoons kosher salt
¾ teaspoon ground pepper
1 ½ cups whole-wheat flour
2 ½ to 3 ½ unbleached all-purpose flour

Topping

A little oil or cooking spray
2 teaspoons sesame seeds
2 teaspoons poppy seeds
1 teaspoon dried thyme
1 teaspoon dried oregano

Boil water. Stir in bulgur wheat. Reduce heat and cook for 15 minutes or until tender; drain. In a large mixing bowl, dissolve yeast in warm milk (110 to 115 degrees F). Add in oats, flax seeds, raw wild honey, eggs, salt, pepper and whole-wheat flour. Beat until smooth. Stir in enough unbleached all-purpose flour to form a soft dough. Turn the dough onto a floured surface and knead for about 6 to 8 minutes. Place in a greased bowl, turning once to coat. Cover the bowl and let the dough rise for 1¼ hours. Punch the dough down slightly. Turn it onto the lightly floured surface again. Divide the dough into 22 pieces, and roll each piece into balls. Arrange 11 balls into two greased round pans.

Lightly brush each roll with oil. Combine sesame seeds, poppy seeds, thyme and oregano. Sprinkle the mixture on top of the rolls. Cover the rolls and let them rise until they double in size (around 40 minutes). Bake the rolls in a 375 degree oven for 18 to 22 minutes. Remove the rolls from the pans and allow them to cool on wire racks.

COMPOUND BUTTERS

Each of these compound butters is made with one stick of softened butter.

Herb Butter

Add 1 teaspoon each of thyme, oregano, basil and parsley to your butter, or add in a couple of tablespoons of whatever chopped herbs you prefer. Rosemary, thyme, parsley and sage are always a nice combination.

You can also use this compound butter to flavor meat, pork, poultry or fish. Simply add on top and bake it in the oven until cooked through. Herbed butter is scrumptious when used to soften bread crumbs, which can be sprinkled over your favorite seafood before baking or broiling.

Cinnamon Butter

Add 2 tablespoons of raw honey or agave nectar and 1 teaspoon ground cinnamon to your stick of softened butter. Cinnamon butter is delicious with my Multigrain Pan Rolls--or just about any type of bread!

Peach, Raspberry or Strawberry Butter

Sauté 1 cup chopped peach, strawberries or raspberries with ½ teaspoon of ground cinnamon, ¼ teaspoon of ground nutmeg and a touch of orange juice. Let it cool, and then fold it into the softened butter. Try sautéing other fruits you like as well. Use your imagination!

Chive Butter

Add 2 tablespoons of chopped chives and ½ teaspoon white wine to one stick of softened butter. This is wonderful on baked potatoes!

Garlic Butter

You can use roasted or blanched garlic for this butter. To roast garlic, use a serrated knife to cut the top of the garlic head off, exposing the tops of the cloves. Place the garlic in a baking pan and drizzle it with a little olive oil. Sprinkle the garlic with just a touch of salt and black pepper. (You can also wrap it in aluminum foil.) Bake the garlic for thirty minutes, or until it's soft and a lightly browned. (I like to roast several heads of garlic at once.) Once cooled, squeeze the roasted garlic out of its skin. Blend one tablespoon of the roasted garlic and one tablespoon of chopped fresh parsley into one stick of softened butter. If you like a little spice add a pinch of cayenne pepper. This is perfect butter for Garlic Bread! You can store excess roasted garlic in a container in the refrigerator.

Lemon or Lime Butter

Add the zest and juice of one lemon or lime and a little salt and pepper to the butter. This particular butter is great with chicken or fish.

My Grandmother's Sour Soup (Caldo Azedo)

In Portugal soups are often the main meal, and this was no exception in my grandmother's home. One of my favorite soups growing up was my grandmother's Caldo Azedo, or Portuguese Sour Soup. My grandmother was never one to waste food, so this recipe came in handy when she had stale bread. This amazing soup is absolutely delicious and just as fun to eat. My grandmother and I would literally break bread together and place our chunks of bread in the bottom of the bowl. I'd watch as my Vavo lovingly poured the homemade soup over the bread. The bread would soak up the broth and you knew it was time to dig in!

1 pound dry red beans, soaked overnight
1 onion, chopped
1 can (8-ounce) tomato sauce
Salt and pepper to taste
2 garlic cloves, minced
½ stick butter
2 sweet potatoes, cubed
2 white potatoes, cubed
2 tablespoons white vinegar
Crusty bread, such as Portuguese or French bread

Clean the beans well, and soak them in water overnight in a large pot. Cook the beans in the same water they were soaked in. Add in onion, garlic, tomato sauce, salt and pepper. Bring the mixture to a boil, then lower the heat, and allow it to simmer for one hour, until the beans are almost done. Add in potatoes and continue to simmer until fork tender. Add in the butter and vinegar. Stir until the butter melts. Serve over torn bread in a bowl.

Mom's Portuguese Style Oven Roast

Growing up my mother and grandmother would make the most tender and flavorful roasted beef, turkey and chicken using this marinade. I find slow roasting a recipe like this to be so comforting! This recipe is perfect for days when I need to be home to do laundry, dust and vacuum. Your home will smell amazing, too, and you'll be ready to eat when this is done!

1 large eye round roast
2 links or 1 pound chourico (a Portuguese smoked sausage) or your favorite spicy smoked sausage
2 cans tomato sauce
2 cans of water
1 large can of beer or 12 ounces of dry white wine (or a mixture of the two)
2 large onions, sliced
1 to 2 tablespoons fresh red crushed pepper or a little dry to taste (called Pimento Moida) or 1 teaspoon dried red crushed pepper
3 tablespoons each garlic and onion powder
Salt to taste
6 russet potatoes, peeled
6 to 8 carrots, peeled

Add the tomato sauce, water, beer, onion and garlic powder, onion slices, red crushed pepper and salt into a large roasting pan. Place the roast into the marinade, turning once or twice to coat. Cover it and set it to marinate in the refrigerator overnight.

When you're ready to cook the roast, cover it with a lid or aluminum foil and bake it in the marinade in a 350 degree F oven. Baste the roast a few times while it cooks. Your cooking time will depend on the size and cut of you roast, but my mother typically slow roasts hers for several hours until it is very tender.

When the roast is almost as tender as you'd like it, add the potatoes and carrots into the pan. Be sure to coat them with your flavorful marinade. Cook the roast without a cover for another thirty minutes or until the vegetables are fork tender.

Move the roast onto a cutting board and allow it to rest. Slice and assemble the beef, potatoes and carrots onto a nice serving platter. Cover the sliced roast and vegetables with foil while you make the gravy.

Pan Gravy

2 cups strained marinade
2 tablespoons cornstarch
2 tablespoons cold water

Heat the marinade in a saucepan.

In a small bowl, combine the cornstarch and cold water. Slowly add the mixture to the heated marinade, stirring constantly until it thickens. Adorn the beef slices with some of the gravy and serve the rest in a gravy bowl.

Tip: My mother, grandmother and I all used this same marinade and method to roast whole chickens, turkeys and pork as well. When a small crowd was expected, we used chicken or turkey breasts in place of whole chickens and turkeys.

Carrot Potato Mash

My mother Mary first enjoyed this carrot potato mash at her sister Rosie's home many years ago. My mother has always loved preparing the Thanksgiving meal, which usually includes this colorful side dish. The addition of carrots adds a nice sweetness, texture and rich color to the mashed potatoes. Tailor-made for special occasions, the dish adds a nice touch to a murder mystery menu.

3 pounds russet potatoes, peeled and cubed (for cooking purposes, it is very important to cut the potatoes all the same size)
2 pounds carrots, peeled and sliced
3 garlic cloves, smashed
1 stick of salted butter, cubed
1 ½ to 2 cup milk, taken out a few minutes early
½ cup sour cream
Kosher or sea salt and pepper, to taste

Place the potatoes, carrots and garlic cloves in a large pan and cover them with cold water. To ensure even cooking, the potatoes and carrots should be uniform in size, and always started in cold water rather than hot. Cook the vegetables just until they're fork tender. Overcooking your potatoes will make them gummy. Once cooked, drain the water from the veggies and place the pot back over a low heat. Keeping the potatoes and carrots over a low heat will ensure that they stay dry, and it will also help heat your butter and milk as you mash.

Add in your milk, butter, salt and black pepper. Adding very cold milk will cause the potatoes seize up, so I like to set my milk on the counter for a few minutes before using it. Mash the potatoes, milk and butter together. I love my electric mixer because I like the texture the carrots add. The texture of your mashed potatoes is entirely up to you. If you prefer more texture, mash them less. If you prefer a smooth consistency, mash them a bit more. You may also add more milk to get a creamier consistency if you'd like.

Dinner is always better when families eat together!

Green Tomato Spice Cake with Brown Butter Icing

This Green Tomato Cake makes the perfect ending to this murder mystery meal. I first made this cake for North Carolina Secretary of State Elaine Marshall. She and I planned an afternoon of shopping and cooking together. We met at the Raleigh Farmer's Market to buy all of the fruits and vegetables needed. We then made our way back to my home to cook up two recipes featuring the produce we'd purchased. Secretary Marshall and I discussed local sustainability, her life as a farmer's daughter and the benefits of buying local fresh ingredients. I surprised her with my Green Tomato Spice Cake, which I created especially for her. Later that evening Secretary Marshall left a very nice comment on the **Cooking with Elise** website declaring my Green Tomato Spice Cake a *"fantastic hit."*

Cake

2 cups unbleached all-purpose flour
2 teaspoons ground cinnamon
½ teaspoon ground ginger
¼ teaspoon ground cloves
½ teaspoon ground mace
½ teaspoon freshly ground nutmeg
1 ½ teaspoons baking soda
2 teaspoons baking powder
1 teaspoon salt
2 to 2 ½ cups green tomato, chopped
¾ cups chopped walnuts, optional
2 tablespoons candied ginger, chopped
2 cups granulated sugar
1½ cups canola oil
4 large eggs
1 teaspoon pure vanilla extract
1 small (8-ounce) can crushed pineapple and its juices

Sift the flour, cinnamon, ginger, cloves, mace, nutmeg, baking soda, powder and salt together into a large bowl. Set the bowl aside. This is a great job for the kiddos to help with! Fold in the green tomatoes, chopped walnuts and ginger and coat with flour mixture.

In a mixer, combine the sugar, eggs, oil and vanilla. Add the dry ingredients and mix them in well. Add crushed pineapple. Pour the batter into a 9 x 13-inch baking pan coated with non-stick cooking spray. Bake the cake in a 350 degree F oven until a toothpick inserted in the center comes out clean--about one hour.

Brown Butter Icing

Browning the butter adds a lovely nutty flavor to this icing. I love this trick because one of my sons is highly allergic to tree nuts, but he can enjoy this.

1 cup salted butter
2 teaspoons pure vanilla extract
2 cups powdered or light brown sugar

While the cake is baking, melt the butter in a small saucepan and stir it until it turns a dark brown color. Allow the butter to cool and then add in the vanilla and sugar. Remove the cake from the oven and frost it immediately.

Did you know? *A little salt enhances the sweetness of desserts. That's why I also like to use salted butter when baking.*

A Medieval Murder Mystery Dinner

A couple of years later it was our dear friend David's 16th birthday. David, who suffered from a rare form of cerebral palsy, had had a very challenging and pain-filled year. We wanted to ensure that his celebration was memorable and special. So we planned a dramatic medieval murder mystery dinner in his honor. We took great delight in planning the menu, writing the play, and creating the invitations and decorations. A local group of performers generously loaned us their beautiful costumes for our guests to use. Each guest received an invitation from the "King," which requested their presence at *Prince David's 16th Birthday Celebration* and informed them of the role they would be playing.

The stage was set. The decorations were up, and the food was prepped. But then . . .

One day before the party, David received the unfortunate news that he would have to go in for surgery right away. The party would have to be postponed.

Very early the next morning, instead of preparing for a great celebration, we followed David's family to the hospital. We knew the surgery was risky, and that David's life and health would be in danger. Overcome with anxiety, Alex and I prayed for our friends, the doctors and everyone who would care for David.

A short time later, a car passed us. My son Alex turned to me and said in amazement, "Mom, did you see that? That car's bumper sticker said 'Trust in the Lord.'" Several minutes later a different car passed us. This time we both saw another "Trust in the Lord" sticker in the back window. We smiled at one another. Just like that, we knew God had a plan, and there was no need to be anxious. We were right--David's surgery was a success.

Several weeks later...

We were all set to pick up David's birthday celebration where we had left off. We had carefully prepared everything to a tee. A medieval cardboard soldier welcomed guests as they arrived. A large wooden sign announcing Prince David's birthday hung on one of the "castle" walls.

As guests entered our home, they were greeted by the sound of a medieval harp. Two handmade flowing purple banners graced the hallway, or "banquet hall."

The banners featured the words *"Be strong in the Lord and in the power of His might"* and *"Eat, Drink and Be Merry"* in graceful calligraphy. The dining room showcased various types of medieval armor such as a sword, a helmet and a shield.

The bright red, orange and yellow paper sconces the boys and I made in the shape of flames lined the walls of our dining room. Fresh greenery, taken from our yard, hung gracefully around our chandelier. Jewel-toned plastic wrap lined the windows, giving them the appearance of stained glass. Flickering light from the setting sun bathed the room in lovely red, blue, green and golden hues.

Our guests arrived in costume and were immediately given their name tags. The Town Crier announced everyone's presence in the banquet hall. The celebration was about to begin!

The dining room table was draped in a gold tablecloth and covered with a colorful medieval throw. On top of the table sat two Sing a Song of Sixpence French Meat Pies. The two pies were set in a large black wrought-iron pie holder and adorned with paper blackbirds. A framed copy of the poem "Sing a Song of Sixpence" was set next to the pies. A large stone baking dish filled with roasted drumsticks with mustard glaze sat next to a large pot of piping hot creamy potato leek soup. A big basket of bread and a warm pot of cheese fondue added an element of do-it-yourself fun to the spread.

As people began to eat, my son Alex (playing the role of the Town Crier) ran into the room and exclaimed there was a threat on the king's life, and it was up to the guests to figure out the culprit. The play had begun! In the end the king was saved and the mystery was solved. Everyone thoroughly enjoyed the evening—especially our guest of honor, David.

I highly encourage you to invite guests to your own medieval mystery dinner. Each member of your family has their own gifts and talents. Involve the whole family in the planning of the party from the decorations, to the writing of the play, to the preparation of the food. I promise, a more enjoyable experience will be difficult to come by!

Herb Buttermilk Biscuits

These biscuits are one of my son Alexander's most favorite recipes. I often make them for him when he returns home from college. Alexander still remembers the first time I made these biscuits. He was eight year old, and because he loves them so much, I've been making them ever since. It still brings a smile to his face--and to mine, too.

2 cups unbleached all-purpose flour
1 tablespoon granulated sugar
2 ½ teaspoons baking powder
½ teaspoon kosher salt
1/3 cup cold butter, cut into pieces
2/3 cup cold milk or buttermilk
2 tablespoon dried Italian seasonings
2 tablespoon grated Parmesan cheese

Some people love diamonds, but I love kitchen tools. I adore the food processor my husband gave me years ago. It makes biscuit making so speedy!

Preheat your oven to 350 degrees F.

In a small bowl, combine the Italian seasoning and Parmesan cheese and set aside.

Use the dough blade of your food processor to incorporate the flour, sugar, baking powder, salt and butter. Pulse a few times until your mixture looks like small peas. Place this mixture in a bowl and add in the buttermilk; mix just until combined.

Add a little flour to your counter and roll out your dough to about 1/2-inch thick. Using a biscuit cutter, cut the dough into 3-inch circles. When cutting out biscuits, be sure to press straight down and lift straight up to remove. Twisting the biscuit cutter will seal the sides and interfere with rising.

Place your biscuits on a baking stone or sheet and sprinkle them with the Italian seasoning and cheese mixture.

Bake for 8 to 10 minutes until fluffy and slightly browned on top.

Creamy Potato Leek Soup

In addition to serving this soup at David's party, I held a cooking class for a group of children living with Cerebral Palsy and their families. This was one of my all-time favorite cooking classes. The parents of these children, who spent a great deal of time in their wheelchairs, looked for activities to do that would engage and educate them but that were also fun and accessible. Even though the children were nonverbal and had great difficulty using their hands, we still had a great deal of fun in the kitchen. Some of the children pressed the button of my food processor while others watched in delight, excited simply to be included in the preparation of their meal.

½ pound bacon, chopped
3 celery stalks, diced
1 large yellow onion, diced
3 leeks, cleaned very well and chopped
3 cloves garlic, minced
8 russet potatoes, peeled and cubed
4 cups low-sodium chicken stock
4 tablespoons salted butter
¼ cup unbleached all-purpose flour
1 cup heavy cream or half-and-half
Salt and pepper to taste
½ cup shredded cheddar for garnish
¼ cup chopped scallions or chives

Cook your bacon until crispy. Remove from pan and set aside.

Add in the chopped celery, onion and leeks and sauté them until tender. Add in the garlic and cook for 1 minute. Add in the potatoes and sauté them for about 4 minutes. Add chicken stock to cover the potatoes. Simmer until the potatoes are fork tender.

In a separate pan, melt the butter and add in the flour, whisking to make a roux. Add in the cream and bring the mixture to a boil. Continue cooking, stirring until thickened. Stir the cream mixture into the potato mixture. Puree half of the soup, and leave the other half chunky for extra texture. Add salt and pepper to taste. Top with shredded cheddar cheese, minced green onions or chives and bacon pieces.

Sing a Song of Sixpence French Meat Pie

I love developing recipes that bring back fond memories of foods my husband enjoyed as a child. My husband Michael grew up in New Bedford, Massachusetts. Many bakeries sold one of his childhood favorites–the meat pie. To his delight, Michael's mom would sometimes bring home a meat pie for dinner.

I was delighted when I mastered the recipe and surprised my husband with it. I thought it made the perfect addition to our medieval murder mystery dinner . . .

"Sing a song of sixpence/ A pocket full of rye/ Four and twenty blackbirds/ Baked in a pie."

Recipe for Double Flaky Pie Crust

2½ cups unbleached all-purpose flour
1 teaspoon kosher salt
1 teaspoon granulated sugar
2 sticks of unsalted butter, chilled and cut into small pieces
1 tablespoon sour cream
4 to 5 tablespoons ice water

Place the flour, salt, and sugar in the bowl of a food processor fitted with a steel blade; pulse to combine. Add the butter to the flour mixture and give the food processor 5 more pulses. Add the shortening and give it another 5 short pulses. Add the sour cream and give 5 final short pulses. Turn the mixture over into a large bowl.

Sprinkle 3 tablespoons of ice water over the mixture. Using a rubber spatula press down on the dough until it sticks together. Add more ice water if needed, one tablespoon at a time.

Pour your pie dough onto a floured counter and knead just a bit until the dough comes together. Divide the dough in half, shape each piece into a ball with your hands and flatten each ball into a disk. Dust each disk lightly with flour, wrap it in plastic and refrigerate it for at least 30 minutes before rolling it out.

To roll out the dough, lightly dust the rolling pin and countertop with a little flour. Using one disk (half the recipe), roll the dough into a circle that measures 2 inches larger than the pie pan you are using. Lightly flour the top of the dough. Fold the dough in half, then in half again. Place the folded dough in the prepared pan and unfold it. Trim the excess dough to half an inch and fold under around the edges. After shaping, chill the dough for at least 30 minutes before filling or baking.

Meat Pie Filling

2 tablespoons vegetable oil

1 large onion, chopped

1 pound ground beef

1 pound ground pork

1 ½ cup mashed potatoes

1 ½ to 2 teaspoons ground allspice

1 teaspoon salt

¼ teaspoon pepper

Pastry for double-crust pie

1 egg, beaten

In a skillet, heat the oil over medium heat. Sauté the beef, pork and onion together until completely cooked. This recipe calls for a filling with a VERY smooth consistency. To achieve this, I run the cooked mixture through my food processor. Once the meat mixture is smooth enough, I mix in the mashed potatoes and spices.

Line a buttered pie plate with one of the pie crusts. Fill the crust with the meat and potato mixture. Cover the pie with the second crust. Seal and flute the pie's edges. Make slits in the top crust to allow steam to escape. Brush the crust with the beaten egg. Bake it at 375 degrees F for 30 to 35 minutes--or until golden brown.

Arroz Doce (Rice Pudding)

In medieval times, rice pudding was a common sweet treat. This creamy, smooth and rich pudding is still delicious enough to please a modern crowd.

One of my favorite desserts of my grandmother's was her rice pudding. Believe me, I could hear that pudding bubble and smell its mild, milky sweetness from a mile away. I loved the pudding's rich yellow color, which contrasted so vibrantly with the cinnamon she sprinkled on top. While I use lemon zest for this recipe, Vavo didn't. Instead she added an entire lemon peel, cut into one long strip, to the milk. I still don't know how she cut that peel! You were very fortunate if you happened to be there when Vavo removed the lemon peel. After simmering away for awhile in the pudding, it would magically transform into a puffy, candy-like treat filled with sugared milk, which we gleefully devoured.

My grandmother didn't use saffron or toasted almonds in her rice pudding. I added these ingredients as a nod to medieval cookery, where almonds were commonly used and saffron, the most expensive spice in the world, was a sign of high social status.

Vavo's rice pudding calls for an abundance of rice, which is cooked until it's tender, yet still firm. Her version is thicker, denser and has more texture than the more custard-like puddings many people are used to, but that's precisely what makes it so amazing!

1 ½ cups arborio rice (the short grain rice used in risotto recipes)
4 cups cold water
Zest of one lemon
Pinch of saffron threads, optional
2 cinnamon sticks
1 teaspoon kosher salt
4 egg yolks
2 cups granulated sugar
3 cups milk
½ teaspoon pure vanilla extract
Ground cinnamon for dusting on top
Toasted coconut and slivered almonds for garnish

In a saucepan, combine the rice, water, lemon zest, saffron threads and salt. Cook the mixture over med/low heat until the rice absorbs the water. Leave the rice a little bit firm, as it will continue to soften in the milk later on.

In a bowl combine the sugar and egg yolks. Mix them well; set aside for later.

Scald the milk in a large saucepan with cinnamon sticks. When the rice is cooked, add it to the milk. Cook the rice and milk for about 5 minutes until it thickens and turns bubbly. Remove the cinnamon sticks. Take a little of the milk and mix it in with the egg yolk and sugar mixture to bring the egg yolks up to temperature so that you don't end up with scrambled eggs!

Add the sugar and egg yolk mixture to the rice and milk mixture and stir well. Leave it on the heat for about 6 to 8 minutes, stirring regularly. It should be creamy, but not too thick. Pour the mixture into a buttered 9 x 13-inch baking pan. Sprinkle ground cinnamon liberally over the top. The pudding will thicken as it sets in refrigerator. Garnish the pudding with toasted coconut and slivered almonds if you'd like. It adds a lovely flavor and texture to the rice. Enjoy!

Notes and Memories

Pancakes

Stacks of Fun Morning, Noon and Night

Homemade Whipped Cream

Mock Maple Syrup

Pumpkin Granola Pancakes

Wholegrain Apple Oat Pancakes

Blueberry Orange and White Chocolate Buttermilk Pancakes

Swedish Pancakes with Cannoli Filling and Chocolate Wine Sauce

Sweet Potato Pancakes with Spiced Nuts

Due to the morning dash, many people do not have time to enjoy a nice sit-down breakfast together. Eating breakfast for dinner is just plain fun! Why not enjoy a nice pancake supper together? Get those pajamas on early and get the whole family involved. Finish up the evening by enjoying a nice family read-aloud or watching a family-friendly movie together! Here are some of our family's favorite pancake recipes.

Homemade Whipped Cream

Once you've tasted and seen how easy it is to make homemade whipped cream you will never purchase another tub of whipped topping again. We've enjoyed this with both our pancakes and our desserts.

1 pint heavy whipping cream
½ cup granulated or powdered sugar
1 teaspoon pure vanilla extract (almond extract is really nice as well)

Pour the cold cream, sugar and vanilla into a chilled mixing bowl. Beat the ingredients until they thicken.

Tip: I sometimes use a couple of drops of liquid Stevia in place of the sugar.

Mock Maple Syrup

Okay, so you just made your favorite pancakes or French toast and realize that you're out of maple syrup. No worries! My preference is always a really good quality pure maple syrup, but this recipe has really come in handy over the years!

1 cup granulated sugar
¼ cup brown sugar
1 cup water
1 teaspoon pure vanilla extract

In a medium saucepan, bring all of the ingredients to a boil. Cover the saucepan for 1 minute. Turn off the heat and let the syrup sit until it thickens.

Pumpkin Granola Pancakes

One of my favorite vegetables is pumpkin. Often underutilized out of season, pumpkin can be found not only fresh during the fall, but throughout the year in the canned goods section of your grocery store.

For a little change, I add a sprinkling of my favorite pumpkin flax granola cereal on top of each pancake. The result is a scrumptious pancake with a unique texture and a nutty flavor! I adorned my pancakes with a bit of pure maple syrup and a dollop of billowy homemade whipped cream.

1 large egg
1½ cups milk
1 cup canned pumpkin (not pie filling)
2 tablespoon canola oil
2 tablespoon apple cider vinegar
½ teaspoon pure vanilla extract
2 cups unbleached all-purpose flour
3 tablespoons light brown sugar
2 teaspoons baking powder
1 teaspoon baking soda
½ teaspoon ground allspice
1 teaspoon ground cinnamon
½ teaspoon freshly ground nutmeg
½ teaspoon ground cloves
½ teaspoon ground ginger
2 tablespoons chopped candied ginger, optional
½ teaspoon kosher salt
1 cup pumpkin granola (We love Nature's Path Organic Pumpkin Flaxseed Plus)
Non-stick cooking spray

In a large bowl whisk together the egg, milk, pumpkin, oil, vinegar and vanilla extract.

In another bowl, combine the flour, brown sugar, baking powder, baking soda, allspice, cinnamon, nutmeg, cloves, ginger, candied ginger and salt.

Mix the wet mixture and the dry mixture together until smooth.

Spray the griddle with a non-stick cooking spray and pour about 1/3 cup of batter onto the hot surface for each pancake. Cook each pancake over medium-high heat for three minutes or so until bubbles form. Sprinkle two tablespoons of granola on top of each pancake. Then turn each pancake over and cook it until the bottom is slightly golden-brown.

Enjoy these pancakes with homemade whipped cream and a sprinkling of ground cinnamon.

It's fun to get together and have something good to eat at least once a day. That's what human life is all about -- enjoying things.

– Julia Child

Wholegrain Apple Oat Pancakes

Aside from prayer, these apple oat pancakes are the best way to start or end your day. As a child, I loved watching my mother make pancakes. I loved seeing the air bubbles form, as I knew that I was only moments away from sinking my teeth into their yummy, fluffy deliciousness.

The currants and apples in this recipe add such a nice natural sweetness to these pancakes. Meanwhile, the toasted pecans add texture and nutty flavor.

Non-stick cooking spray
½ cup rolled oats, ground in food processor
½ cup whole wheat flour
1 cup unbleached all-purpose flour
1 teaspoon aluminum-free baking powder
1 teaspoon baking soda
½ teaspoon ground cinnamon
½ teaspoon ground ginger
½ teaspoon ground mace
½ teaspoon kosher salt
2 large eggs
2 tablespoons olive oil
2 tablespoons agave nectar
1 teaspoon pure almond or vanilla extract
1 ½ cups milk
1 ½ teaspoons of apple cider vinegar
1 apple, peeled, cored and diced into small pieces
2 tablespoons currants

Garnish

Pure maple syrup
Homemade whipped cream
Ground cinnamon

In a large bowl combine the oats, flours, baking powder, soda, cinnamon, ginger, mace and salt.

In another bowl whisk together the eggs, olive oil, agave nectar, almond or vanilla extract, milk and vinegar.

Add the wet ingredients to the dry ingredients and stir until combined.

Spray your griddle with a non-stick cooking spray (I like to use my cast iron griddle). Ladle some of the batter onto the griddle for each pancake. Get your family in the kitchen to help you place some of the chopped apple and currants on top of the pancakes. Wait to flip your pancakes until you see bubbles begin to form, but watch for browning on the bottom-turn your heat up or down accordingly.

Top your pancakes with some pure maple syrup and enjoy.

Blueberry Orange and White Chocolate Buttermilk Pancakes

Reading aloud was always a huge part of our family's daily life. We especially enjoyed the books Laura Ingalls Wilder so lovingly wrote. Laura's heartwarming and amusing stories in the Little House series provided our family with a unique glimpse into pioneer life.

Way back when my boys were around the ages of seven and four, we were all snuggled in bed under the covers reading Little House in the Big Woods aloud when a thick winter snow began to fall.

The boys and I excitedly looked out the window. Soon everything was covered in a thick white blanket of snow.

In one chapter Laura writes about making "Pancake Men" with her mom, Caroline. The boys and I proceeded to our little kitchen to get cookin'!

Although these tiny Pancake Men no longer satisfy my grown sons' appetites, they still enjoy a heaping stack of buttermilk pancakes made with love! Not long ago, my son Alexander and I came up with this winning combination using blueberries, orange and white chocolate.

Pancakes

1 large egg
2 tablespoons oil or butter, melted
2 tablespoons raw honey or agave nectar
1½ cups low fat buttermilk
½ teaspoon pure almond extract (you can use pure vanilla extract, too)
Zest of one orange
1½ cups all-purpose flour
2 teaspoons baking powder
1 teaspoon baking soda
½ teaspoon kosher salt
1 cup fresh blueberries
½ cup white chocolate chips

Orange Maple Syrup

1 cup pure maple syrup
Peel of one large orange

In a small saucepan, bring the maple syrup and orange peel to a boil. Turn off the heat and set the syrup aside.

In a small bowl, whisk together the egg, butter, honey or agave nectar, buttermilk, almond extract and orange zest.

In another bowl, mix together the dry ingredients. Combine the dry and wet ingredients together and mix them well. Let the batter stand for five minutes. If you find the batter too thick to pour, simply thin out with a little water.

Heat a pan to medium-high heat. Coat the pan with non-stick cooking spray. Pour small amounts of batter into the pan. Place blueberries and white chocolate chips on top of each pancake. Cook each pancake until little bubbles form on the surface, and then turn each over to complete the cooking process. Enjoy with a drizzle of orange maple syrup.

Swedish Pancakes with Cannoli Filling and Chocolate Wine Sauce

This crepe recipe is perfect for dessert or a special brunch.

Begin by making your cannoli filling:

Cannoli Filling

2 cups ricotta cheese put into a cheese cloth or a strainer
1 cup powdered sugar
Zest of one large orange or lemon
½ teaspoon pure almond extract
½ cup miniature chocolate chips

In a mixing bowl combine ricotta cheese, powdered sugar, orange zest, almond extract and miniature chocolate chips.

Set aside in the refrigerator. Now make your Chocolate Wine Sauce:

Chocolate Wine Sauce

½ cup half and half
1 tablespoon softened butter
1/3 cup muscadine wine or your favorite sweet red wine
2 cups semi-sweet chocolate chips
1 teaspoon vanilla extract
2 teaspoon agave nectar
½ teaspoon ground cinnamon
Pinch of fresh nutmeg

Combine all ingredients in a medium saucepan. Stir well. Bring to a boil, reduce heat and simmer, uncovered, for 8-10 minutes, until slightly thickened. Remove from heat and set aside to thicken.

Now prepare your crepe batter:

3 large eggs
2½ cups milk, divided in half
1¼ cup unbleached all-purpose flour
½ teaspoon kosher salt
3 tablespoons butter, melted
1 teaspoon pure vanilla extract
Non-stick butter spray
Slivered almonds for garnish

Whisk together eggs, half of the milk, the butter, and half of the flour. Add the remaining milk and the vanilla extract and the remaining flour and salt and mix well.

Spray a round non-stick pan with butter spray. The size of your crepe will depend on the size of your pan. Add about a ½ cup of batter, move the batter around to coat your pan.

Let the crepe cook until bubbles form. Turn the entire pancake over and let it cook one minute more. Do not make the pancake too thick.

To serve, place a bit of the delicious cannoli filling in the middle of your crepe and fold both sides over. Drizzle chocolate wine sauce over top and garnish with toasted almonds.

Sweet Potato Pancakes adorned with Spiced Nuts

I first enjoyed sweet potato pancakes with spiced nuts at Tupelo Honey's, a wonderful local restaurant in downtown Asheville, North Carolina. Once I moved to Raleigh, I had to come up with my own creation because I loved them so much.

Begin by making your Spiced Nuts. I always make a large batch of these nuts. I store the spiced nuts in a container to top off my salads, to snack on, or to give as a gift.

Spiced Pecans

1 large egg white
1 cup granulated sugar
2 teaspoons ground cinnamon
1 teaspoon freshly ground nutmeg
¼ teaspoon ground ginger
¼ teaspoon ground cloves
¼ teaspoon ground allspice
2 cups unsalted pecans or your favorite nut

Preheat oven to 350 degrees F.

In a large mixing bowl beat the egg white lightly. In another bowl stir together sugar, cinnamon, nutmeg, ginger, cloves, and allspice and mix well. Add the pecans to the whipped egg white and coat them completely. Next coat the pecans completely in the cinnamon and sugar mixture and place them in a single layer on a parchment-lined baking sheet.

I like using the bottom of my broiler pan so the nuts don't fall off while baking. Bake them for 25 to 30 minutes, stirring half way through until the sugar coating is crisp.

Tip: Great in salads, these spiced nuts will last quite a while in an air-tight container. They make the perfect gift, too!

Sweet Potato Pancake Batter

2 cups unbleached all-purpose flour
3 tablespoons light brown sugar
2 teaspoons baking powder
1 teaspoon baking soda
1 teaspoon ground allspice
1 teaspoon ground cinnamon
½ teaspoon ground ginger
¼ teaspoon ground nutmeg
½ teaspoon kosher salt
1½ cups milk
1 cup sweet potato puree
1 large egg
2 tablespoons olive oil
2 tablespoons apple cider vinegar

Combine all the ingredients and whisk them together well. If your batter is too thick, just add a little water.

Pour small amounts of batter onto the griddle. Cook the pancakes over medium-high heat. Once bubbles form, turn them over and cook them for a minute or two longer.

Enjoy these pancakes with real maple syrup, homemade whipped cream, cinnamon, and spiced nuts.

Variation: Use pumpkin puree (not pie filling) in place of sweet potato puree.

Cinnamon Roll Pancakes

Prepare yourself for pure delight, squeals of glee, and requests for more! This is a dessert to remember!

Cinnamon Roll Filling

½ cup salted butter, melted
¾ cup packed brown sugar
1 tablespoon ground cinnamon

In a small saucepan, melt together the butter, brown sugar and cinnamon. Place the butter mixture in a bowl and set it aside to cool for a few minutes. Once cooled, place it in a freezer bag.

Pancake Batter

1 large egg
2 tablespoons melted butter or canola oil
2 tablespoons granulated sugar
1½ cups buttermilk
1½ cups all-purpose flour
2 teaspoons baking powder
1 teaspoon baking soda
½ teaspoon kosher salt
2 tablespoons warm water

In a large bowl, whisk together the egg, melted butter, sugar and buttermilk.

In a small bowl, combine the flour, baking powder, baking soda and salt. Add this dry mixture to the wet egg mixture and combine them just until mixed. Thin the batter with the water. Set the batter aside while you make the icing.

Icing

4 tablespoons softened butter
2 cups powdered sugar
1½ teaspoon pure vanilla extract
4 to 6 tablespoons milk

Combine all four ingredients. Set the icing aside.

Cut the tip of the freezer bag that contains the cooled cinnamon filling. Because the butter will separate, you will have to squish the filling around in the bag a bit to mix it up again.

Spray a cast iron skillet with non-stick cooking spray. Pour small amounts of batter into the pan. Cook the pancakes over medium-high heat. Squeeze the cinnamon filling out of the freezer bag, swirling it around the pancakes. Turn the pancakes over once bubbles form and cook them for one more minute, or until they're golden-brown.

After you cook each batch of pancakes, wipe the griddle with paper towels so the sugar will not harden.

Drizzle icing over the top and get your fork ready!

Note: We sometimes put fresh orange zest in our icing.

Notes and Memories

Chinese Take In

Steamed Dumplings

Fresh Lettuce Wraps

Chinese Egg Rolls

Asian Chicken Kabobs

Chicken Fried Rice

Fortune Cookies

Almond Cookies

Some of my most favorite Cooking with Elise segments featured on the My Carolina Today show were those that included my family. My husband once joined me for a special Mother's Day segment. He and I made multigrain waffles with blueberry syrup together. My youngest son Alexander once joined in the fun as we shared our Chicken Tikka Masala recipe with the viewers. My oldest son Nathaniel and I made Steamed Dumplings with Nate's Dipping Sauce and our specialty egg rolls – two of our favorite Chinese recipes. You can view our family's segments online at cookingwithelise.com.

My son Nathaniel is fifty percent Chinese and so our family has always celebrated the Chinese New Year annually. My children grew up saying, **"Gong Hey Fat Choy"** which means "Happy New Year" in Cantonese. When the boys were younger we always took the opportunity to invite close friends and family to our home to celebrate the Chinese New Year with us.

One year the boys and I made a very elaborate Chinese dragon. We used a vast array of colors to adorn a large box, which became the head of the dragon. We cut flaps out of the box so that a child could easily fit inside. The head was decorated with brightly colored green, blue, red and yellow tissue paper, and had a huge mouth with red, yellow and orange flames protruding from it. A large white sheet painted in bright red and yellow made up the dragon's body.

The boys distributed homemade flyers throughout our New York neighborhood. The next day, our neighbors watched as our family and friends paraded the dragon around the neighborhood. We carried noisemakers and some even wore costumes. One friend and her three boys made a very sophisticated dragon out of wooden slats and he, too, was paraded around the block.

Our dragon made his appearance each January or February around the time of the Chinese New Year. It even emerged once at a local children's story time. After the boys paraded the dragon around, they read one of their favorite books, "The Empty Pot," to the younger children.

In preparation for one Chinese New Year Party, my husband created a fun and engaging way to introduce the children to pi, a number that represents the ratio of the circumference of a circle to its diameter (See page 107). Approximately equal to 3.14, pi is one of the most important mathematical and physical constants used in mathematics, science and engineering. Although the Chinese were not responsible for finding pi, they did make great strides in computing it. During our party, we held a pi reciting contest, used circular plates to demonstrate pi, and showed the children how to convert things into pi, including their next pi birthday!

Steamed Dumplings

My boys and I love to make these dumplings steamed or fried. I generally think the steamed kind is much better. We always serve them with the delicious dipping sauce my son Nathaniel developed. There's nothing quite as nice as having the whole family in the kitchen together. One of the reasons we bought our home is because our kitchen, keeping room and eating area are one big room. Even if we're not cooking together, we all seem to congregate in the kitchen.

Dumplings

2 pounds ground pork
2 tablespoons low sodium soy sauce
2 teaspoons garlic powder
2 teaspoons onion powder
½ teaspoon kosher salt

Combine the ground pork, soy sauce, garlic powder, onion powder and salt. Turn each wonton wrapper so that it's shaped like a diamond. Place a good tablespoon or so of the pork mixture in the middle of each wonton. Moisten the edges of the wontons with water, connect opposite points to seal.

Using a steamer, cook the wontons for 10 to 12 minutes.

Nate's Delicious Dipping Sauce

2 tablespoons low sodium soy sauce
1 tablespoon rice vinegar
1 tablespoon toasted sesame oil
1 tablespoon low sodium teriyaki sauce
A good shake of dried red crushed pepper, depending on your taste
1 teaspoon lemon juice
½ teaspoon garlic powder

Combine all ingredients and serve them with your dumplings!

Fresh Lettuce Wraps

3 tablespoons low sodium soy sauce
1 tablespoon teriyaki sauce
2 teaspoon sesame oil
½ teaspoon garlic powder
1 teaspoon onion powder
2 teaspoons brown sugar
Pinch of dried red pepper flakes (about 1/8 of a teaspoon)
1 package of Asian rice noodles, also known as rice sticks or vermicilli
1 tablespoon sesame oil
3 boneless chicken breasts, diced into small pieces
1 tablespoon sesame oil
1 (8-ounce) can sliced water chestnuts, diced
One bunch scallions, chopped
Boston or iceberg lettuce, leaves pulled apart, washed and dried

In a small bowl, combine the soy sauce, teriyaki sauce, two teaspoons of sesame oil, garlic and onion powders, brown sugar and red crushed pepper flakes. Set aside.

Boil your rice noodles for three minutes in salted water. Drain them well and stir fry them with a tablespoon of sesame oil in a wok or large skillet until a little crispy. Set the noodles aside.

In the same wok or large skillet, sauté the chicken in a tablespoon of sesame oil over high heat for about five minutes. Add in the scallions and water chestnuts. Stir fry the whole mixture for one minute more. Add in your sauce and cook the chicken for five more minutes, or until the sauce has reduced by half and becomes thicker.

We enjoy serving everything you need to make your lettuce wraps on a large platter. That way, friends and family can have fun making their own wraps. To assemble your wraps, place some of the crispy noodles inside the lettuce leaf, top with the chicken and enjoy.

Chicken and Vegetable Egg Rolls

1 package egg roll wrappers (you can find these in the refrigerated section of your grocery store)
3 boneless chicken breasts, cut into tiny pieces
1/3 cup dry sherry
1/3 cup low-sodium soy sauce
2 teaspoons granulated
3 tablespoons toasted sesame oil
4 carrots, grated
1 green bell pepper, diced
2 cloves garlic, minced
Salt and pepper to taste
Peanut or grapeseed oil

Add the sherry, soy sauce and sugar to a plastic container or plastic storage bag. Add your chicken pieces to the container or bag, seal it tightly and let it marinate for least 30 minutes in the refrigerator. Always place bags of marinating meat, pork or poultry on a plate or in a bowl to prevent possible leaking all over your refrigerator.

Heat 2 tablespoons of the sesame oil in a skillet. Add in the carrots and green pepper. Cook them until they're tender and a bit caramelized. Add in the garlic and cook it in with the vegetables for 2 minutes. Remove the vegetables and set them aside. Add one more tablespoon of sesame oil to the pan. Cook the chicken until it's done--approximately 5 to 6 minutes. Add the chicken to the bell peppers, carrots, and garlic. Season the mixture with a little salt and pepper and let it cool.

Place an egg roll wrapper so that it looks like a diamond. Spread 2 tablespoons of the filling across the widest part of the wrapper. Take the point facing you and fold it over the mixture. Tightly fold both sides inward and complete rolling. Use a little water on the final point before closing the egg roll wrapper completely.

Heat the peanut or grapeseed oil in a deep saucepan and fry the egg wrappers until they're browned. Because the filling is already cooked, you are just cooking the wrapper itself. Be sure to have your heat high enough (375 degrees F). If the egg rolls don't cook quickly, they will become soggy. Make sure you don't overcrowd the pan.

Tips for Making Egg Rolls

1. You can freeze the marinade and chicken in a heavy-duty freezer bag and thaw the mixture when you're ready to make your egg rolls.
2. Drain the oil from the chicken and vegetables so the wrappers don't get soggy.
3. You must allow the filling to cool before adding it to the egg roll wrapper.
4. Make sure you taste the filling before you put it in the wrappers; that way you can adjust the seasonings if needed.
5. Frying egg rolls as soon as they are filled prevents them from getting soggy.
6. Make the filling ahead of time.
7. If you can, use peanut oil and bring the temperature to 375 degrees F. Peanut oil has a higher smoke point than most oils.
8. Heating oil changes its characteristics. Some oils can become unhealthy when heated too high, so make sure you find out which are best to use when frying. Peanut oil is a great choice, but you can try grapeseed oil if anyone in your family is allergic to peanuts.
9. Place only two egg rolls in the pan at a time. Overcrowding can cause splattering and can bring the oil temperature down too far.
10. Never stack egg rolls on top of one another before or after frying.

FAMILY FUN

This is a fun and engaging way to introduce children to pi.

Materials Needed

A circular object (like a paper plate)
String
Scissors
Tape

To Do and Notice

Carefully wrap a string around the *circumference* of your circular object. (Ask a partner to help.) Cut the string when it is exactly the same length as the circumference. Now take your "string circumference" and stretch it across the *diameter* of your circular object. Cut as many "string diameters" from your "string circumference" as you can. How many diameters could you cut? Compare your data with others. What do you notice?

What's Going On?

This is a hands-on way to divide a circle's circumference by its diameter. No matter what circle you use, you'll be able to cut 3 complete diameters and have a small bit of string left over. Tape the 3 + pieces of string onto paper and explain their significance. Estimate what fraction of the diameter the small piece of leftover string could be (about 1/7). You have now completed the same exercise that people used thousands of years ago when they were curious about the mathematical properties of circles!

Asian Chicken Kabobs

My husband Michael and son Alexander were excited to accompany me to my very first media appearance on Charlotte Today. My oldest son Nathaniel was unfortunately unable to join us due to his summer work schedule. As we traveled back home, Nathaniel called and said, "Mom, don't worry about stopping on the way to eat." He was making something special for dinner.

After a day of traveling, we had a wonderful homemade meal **made with love** waiting for us. Nathaniel had made beautiful, fragrant grilled chicken kabobs. He had used three types of marinades for the chicken! All of them were delicious, but everyone agreed that the Asian Chicken Kabobs were definitely our favorite. I never take my family for granted—they are such a blessing to me!

2 pounds boneless chicken breasts, trimmed of any fat and cut into large cubes
1 cup Hoisin sauce
½ cup low-sodium soy sauce
½ cup Worcestershire sauce
2 tablespoons sesame oil

You will need wood or metal skewers for this recipe. If you're using wood skewers, soak them while the chicken is marinating. Soaking prevents the skewers from burning on the grill.

Add the sesame oil, Hoisin, soy, and Worcestershire sauces, and chicken into a large plastic food storage bag. Place the bag into a bowl in the refrigerator. The longer the chicken stays in the marinade, the better flavor it will have. Nate allowed the chicken to marinate for a couple of hours.

Place the chicken on the skewers and place the skewers on your outdoor grill or under the broiler. Don't overcrowd the skewers. Cook the chicken for ten minutes--just until the juices run clear. Nate is so much better at grilling chicken than I am. He knows exactly when to take it off of the heat. It is always juicy and moist and has the perfect grill flavor.

TIP: Nathaniel also grilled zucchini and yellow squash. Because poultry and vegetables cook at different times, the vegetables went on their own skewers. To insure proper cooking, you should never crowd your skewers whether cooking poultry, meat or vegetables.

Chicken Fried Rice

Makes 6 hearty portions

In the time it takes to pick up your order from a Chinese restaurant, you could have this rice ready to serve--and at a fraction of the cost! This is a great recipe to use with leftover chicken.

4 cups cooked white rice, room temperature or cold
4 eggs, beaten
¼ cup toasted sesame oil
2 boneless chicken breasts, cut into small pieces
1 yellow onion, chopped
3 tablespoons plus 1/3 cup low-sodium soy sauce
2 tablespoons sesame seeds
1 cup frozen peas, optional

Add the sesame oil to a wok or large pan over high heat. Cook the beaten eggs for just a minute and then remove them from the pan. Cook the chicken until it's done. Add in the onion and cook it for one minute. Add in 3 tablespoons of soy sauce. Add in the rice and toasted sesame seeds. Cook the mixture for a few more minutes, stirring constantly. Add in the last 1/3 cup of soy sauce. Finally, add in the peas and cooked egg. Remove the rice from the heat and serve!

Chinese Food for Christmas?

Watching the 1983 Christmas comedy film, "A Christmas Story" has become a family tradition in our home. One of our favorite parts in the movie is when the door is left open allowing the Bumpuses' hounds (who frequently torment Ralphie's father) to eat the family's Christmas turkey, which was left unattended to cool on the table.

Ralphie's father decides to take his family out to eat Christmas dinner. Thankfully, "The Chop Suey Palace" is opened on Christmas Day. The waiters sing the Christmas carols off-key for the family. "Fa ra ra ra ra ra ra ra ra!" The waiters did their best (which I love) and even with the owner's attempts at correction, the waiters continue to pronounce the notes incorrectly…fa ra ra ra ra ra ra ra ra!

For the main course, rather than a turkey, the family is treated to a duck. In accordance to Chinese custom, the duck is served with the head intact. When the father mentions that the duck is "smiling" at him, the cook swiftly and efficiently hacks the head off with a cleaver right in front of the family. I get hysterical just thinking about it! I love how they had a hilarious time dining on duck which Ralphie called their "Chinese turkey."

Like most Chinese restaurants, I'm sure the Chop Suey Palace gave Ralphie's family fortune cookies at the end of their Christmas meal. Our family has our own recipe for Chinese Fortune Cookies, so we can top off our at-home Chinese meals properly!

Fortune Cookies

1 egg white
½ teaspoon pure vanilla extract
½ teaspoon pure almond extract
1 pinch salt
¼ cup unbleached whole wheat flour
Zest of one lemon
2 tablespoons granulated sugar

Preheat your oven to 350 degrees F. Spray a baking stone or sheet with non-stick cooking spray. Write a personal message on 4-inch by ½-inch strips of paper.

Mix the egg white, vanilla, almond and lemon zest until the mixture is foamy but not stiff.

Sift the flour, salt and sugar together and blend them into the egg white mixture.

Place teaspoonfuls of batter at least 4 inches apart on your cookie sheet. Using the back of a small spoon, spread the batter so that you have a circle approximately 3 inches in diameter. Do not make too many at one time. You must form them as soon as they come out of the oven—once they cool, they become brittle.

Bake the cookies for 5 minutes, or until just the outer edges turn golden brown. Remove each cookie with a spatula and place your message in the center. Fold the cookie over to form a fortune cookie shape and place in an egg carton or mini-muffin tin to harden.

Almond Cookies

1 cup salted butter, softened
1 cup granulated sugar
1 large egg
1 ½ teaspoons pure almond extract
2 ¾ cups unbleached all-purpose flour
½ teaspoon kosher salt
½ teaspoon baking soda
Slivered almonds

Preheat the oven to 350 degrees.

Mix together the butter, sugar, egg, and extract until they're smooth.

Sift the dry ingredients together. Add the dry mixture to the wet egg mixture and stir until a dough forms.

Roll the dough into small balls. Place the balls on an ungreased cookie sheet or stone and press three or four slivered almonds on top. Bake the cookies for 10 to 12 minutes or until they're golden brown--but remember, cookies harden as they cool so be sure to take them out before they are fully cooked.

Notes and Memories

An Afternoon Tea or brunch

Mom's Best Chicken Salad Sandwiches

Roasted Asparagus Quiches

Everything but the Kitchen Sink Breakfast Pudding

Strawberries and Cream Scones

No-Recipe-Needed Orange Glaze

Pumpkin Ginger Spice Muffins

Pumpkin Chip Scones

Peanut Butter Banana Muffin Tops

Berry Parfaits

I am so grateful for the example my parents and grandmother set for me. Growing up I was taught that a person shows who he is by what he does and not by what he has. Caring for others, no matter how much or little you may have, is something I learned at a very young age. Waking up with a purpose is the best feeling in the world.

I love hosting tea parties and brunches in my home especially to show appreciation for treasured friends who have been instrumental with community fundraisers and projects.

I believe that those who reach deep down within themselves to faithfully serve others bring forth spiritual fruit and plant seeds of the Spirit. For this reason, at my tea parties and brunches I give friends a particular flower, fruit or spice specifically chosen to match their personalities. During one afternoon tea, a dear friend who is very compassionate received a gift of allspice, while another received a packet of Bluebell seeds for her constant help and support during a project. In addition, each place setting included the friend's name, a picture of the flower, fruit or seed and the plant's meaning.

My parents visited during the summer of 2004, so I arranged a special luncheon for my mom and my friend Peachie. After visiting a beautiful tea room in Asheville, North Carolina, I knew it was the perfect place to spend an afternoon with my special visitors.

The tea room owner's love for her mother and grandmother was unmistakable. Under each glass table were old black and white family photographs, napkins crocheted by her grandmother and other family treasures. This tea room radiated love and light and I knew it was the perfect place to share with my mom and friend.

When I made my reservation I mentioned that my mother and friend would be visiting from Massachusetts and how much I wished to do something meaningful for my mother.

Our tea party took place on a beautiful, sunny, summer day. The sun was shining and we all wore lovely sundresses. Upon our arrival we were taken to a special table by the window. The table was beautifully adorned with flowers, and pretty satchels were tied around the back of each chair just for us. This delightful afternoon is now a special memory for all three of us.

Although my mother has never been here in person for one of my tea parties or brunches, she is always here in spirit. In her honor, her beloved Chicken Salad Sandwiches always sit at the center of our family table.

Mom's Chicken Salad Sandwiches

I love using orange-scented dish detergent, because every time I wash my dishes I seem to be transported back to my parent's kitchen. Don't you just love how our five senses can do that?

Living very far away from family, I value the familiar smells and tastes of my childhood. This is certainly no different when making and eating my mother's Chicken Salad Sandwiches, one of my childhood favorites.

Mom's sandwiches are known, not only throughout Massachusetts, but in every city and town I've ever lived in. I have fond memories of my mother and me making these sandwiches in the kitchen together.

As I grew up, my Mom would make these sandwiches for many family gatherings. I'd sometimes help her chop up the chicken very finely, fill the tiny, soft New England rolls or sprinkle each sandwich with a little paprika for color. Today, I use my coveted food processor, not only for ease and time's sake, but because I can never chop my chicken as finely by hand as I can in the food processor, and that is the secret to these delicious sandwiches! Everyone loves the flavor and smooth consistency of this chicken salad.

Want to get a head start on your party preparations? You can make the chicken salad several days in advance and store it in the refrigerator.

4 boneless or bone-in chicken breasts
3 stalks celery
1 onion, quartered
2 tablespoons onion powder
2 teaspoons garlic powder
1 to 2 teaspoons kosher salt to taste
1 teaspoon ground black pepper
1 cup or so mayonnaise
Paprika for garnish

Place your chicken breasts in a pot and cover them with water. Add in the celery and onion. Bring water to a boil and then lower the temperature. Simmer the chicken until it's cooked through and tender. The cooking time will vary depending on whether you use boneless or bone in chicken breasts. Bone in chicken will take a little longer to cook. Do not overcook the chicken--keeping it moist is the key.

Once the chicken is cooked, allow it to cool. If you're using bone-in chicken, pull all of the meat from the bones. Using a sharp knife or a food processor, chop the chicken into very, very fine pieces.

Add in the salt, pepper, garlic power, onion powder and mayonnaise. Add in enough mayo to make the salad creamy, but not so much that overpowers the chicken. Mix the ingredients well. Place chicken salad into your favorite soft rolls and sprinkle tops with a little paprika for color and additional flavor.

Roasted Asparagus Quiche

What an attractive quiche this makes. Laying the asparagus on top of the egg mixture in a pretty pattern lets your guests know how much you care for them. I bet you won't even miss the crust --it's that delicious!

2 tablespoons butter
2 bunches asparagus spears
Drizzle of olive oil
1 teaspoon kosher salt
½ teaspoon ground black pepper
Zest of one large lemon
1 dozen large eggs
1 cup half-and-half
½ teaspoon freshly ground nutmeg
1 bunch scallions, chopped
1 cup grated Parmesan cheese

Preheat your oven to 400 degrees.

Butter a 9 x 13-inch baking pan and set aside.

Cut the bottoms of your washed and dried asparagus by approximately 2 inches. Place your spears on a large baking sheet or use the bottom of your broiler pan as I do. Coat your spears with a little olive oil and season them with salt and pepper. Toss them well in the seasoning. Bake the asparagus on the top rack of your oven for about 10 minutes, or until your spears are cooked but still have a bite to them. You never want to overcook your vegetables, particularly because these will be baked in the quiche and will therefore cook up further.

While your asparagus is roasting in the oven, begin building your quiche. In a large bowl, mix the eggs, half-and-half, ground nutmeg, chopped scallions and Parmesan cheese together.

As soon as the asparagus is removed from the oven, zest one large lemon over top.

Cut half of your asparagus into 2-inch pieces. Reserve the remaining whole stalks for later. Add the cut pieces of roasted asparagus to your egg mixture and pour the mixture into your prepared pan. Place your baking pan in front of you horizontally. Arrange each piece of asparagus vertically on top of the quiche, alternating the top and bottom direction of each piece. Place the quiche into the oven and bake it for 35 minutes or until a toothpick inserted in the center comes out clean.

Everything but the Kitchen Sink Breakfast Pudding

Do you have a little bit of this and a little piece of that? You can use leftovers to make a delicious savory breakfast pudding that your family and friends will adore! This hearty recipe can be made the night before and will feed a whole crowd!

This pudding calls for breakfast sausage and bacon. However, you can make a lovely version using leftover turkey or chicken and chopped apples, onions, sage and thyme. Another option is to use leftover corned beef, potatoes and carrots. Smoked Cajun sausage, peppers and onions would be wonderful, too! Add in your favorite cheese and mix and match. Encourage your family to use their imaginations!

2 teaspoons extra virgin olive oil

8 ounces breakfast sausage links, cut into bite size pieces

4 pieces cooked bacon (we love turkey bacon)

½ cup cooked ham, chopped

½ green bell pepper, minced

½ red bell pepper, minced

3 cloves garlic, minced

1 loaf of French or Italian bread, cubed (approximately 8 cups)

8 eggs

3 cups whole milk

½ cup heavy cream

1½ teaspoons Slap Ya Mama or a mixture of salt, pepper and garlic powder

Topping

2 tablespoons butter, melted

1 cup grated cheddar or your choice

½ cup grated pecorino Romano cheese

Brown the sausage in a little olive oil. Transfer it onto a plate lined with paper towels. Add the ham, onions and bell peppers and cook them until the peppers and onions are tender—about 5 minutes. Add in the garlic and cook the mixture for 2 more minutes. Remove the mixture from the heat and allow it to cool.

In a large bowl, whisk together the eggs, milk, heavy cream and spices.

Place your bread cubes in a large 9 x 13-inch baking pan. Add in the meat and vegetable mixture and toss it together. Add in the egg mixture. Bake the pudding in a 350 degree F oven for 50 to 55 minutes.

In the meantime, melt the butter and add in the bread crumbs. Brown the buttered bread crumbs for just a minute or so. Let them cool and add in grated cheese.

After the pudding has cooked for 55 minutes, sprinkle the bread crumbs on top, and then cook it for an additional 15 to 20 minutes. Enjoy!

Strawberries and Cream Scones

I have very happy memories of afternoons spent with my children at various pick-your-own farms in both New York and North Carolina. In the fall we would pick various kinds of apples and pumpkins. In the spring we loved to pick fresh strawberries and blueberries. Here in Raleigh we have a pick-your-own strawberry farm very close to our home. One spring while my sister, brother-in-law and niece were visiting, our families spent an afternoon walking through the strawberry field. We picked so many berries that day! Later that afternoon we made a very creamy strawberry ice cream together.

I adore scones of all kinds, and I love developing new scone recipes for special occasions: afternoon teas; a special St. Patrick's Day snack; Easter breakfast; or a weekend brunch. I recently created this wonderful strawberries and cream scone recipe for the spring issue of the North Carolina Farm Bureau Magazine. It's the perfect vehicle for freshly-picked strawberries.

Makes 8 large or 16 smaller scones

2 cups unbleached all-purpose flour
3 tablespoons brown sugar
2 teaspoons baking powder
½ teaspoon kosher salt
½ teaspoon baking soda
¼ cup cold butter, cut into pieces
1 cup diced fresh strawberries
Zest and juice of one large orange
1 cup heavy whipping cream
1 large egg yolk
1 teaspoon pure almond extract
Raw sugar for top of scones

Preheat your oven to 400 degrees F. In a food processor combine the flour, brown sugar, baking powder, baking soda and salt. Pulse the mixture a couple of times. Add the pieces of cold butter and pulse again until the mixture resembles coarse crumbs. Pour the mixture into a large bowl. Toss in the beautiful diced strawberries and the aromatic orange zest.

In a measuring cup, combine the whipping cream, egg yolk and almond extract. Add this wet mixture to the dry mixture and stir it with a fork just until combined. Be sure to not over mix. The dough will appear dry, but is not. Turn the dough onto a floured board or counter. This is where the fun begins! Gently press the dough together until it can be easily kneaded. Don't you just love the feeling of dough? Knead the dough about ten times, or until it is nearly smooth. Roll the dough out into an 8-inch circle. Cut the circle into 8 wedges.

Place the scones on a greased baking stone or cookie sheet. Sprinkle raw sugar over the top of each scone. Bake the scones for 10 to 12 minutes, or until they're lightly browned on top. It is fun for children (and you too) to watch the scones "puff up" in the oven. They do so because once the dry acid in the baking powder is added to wet ingredients it begins produce carbon dioxide bubbles, just like yeast.

While the scones are baking, make your glaze.

No-Recipe-Needed Orange Glaze

Juice of one orange
A little pure vanilla extract (approximately ½ teaspoon or so)
Enough powdered sugar to form a glaze (this will depend on the size of your orange)

In a small bowl, combine the fresh orange juice and vanilla extract. Add a little bit of powdered sugar at a time until you reach a good consistency for drizzling. Once the scones are removed from the oven, transfer them to a cooling rack with a piece of parchment or wax paper underneath for easy clean up. Drizzle the glaze over top. This glaze will dry in just a few short minutes. Serve the scones with homemade whipped cream.

Pumpkin Spice Muffins

Warning: The Spice Glaze for these muffins is irresistible, and the addition of orange peel and candied ginger makes them the perfect treat for any Ladies Tea or brunch! Pumpkin-lovers beware! It's almost impossible to eat just one!

Muffins

1½ cups unbleached all-purpose flour
¼ teaspoon of salt
1 cup granulated sugar
1 teaspoon baking soda
½ cup chopped walnuts, optional
3 tablespoons candied ginger
1 cup pumpkin purée
½ cup olive, canola or walnut oil
2 eggs, beaten
¼ cup water
½ teaspoon nutmeg
½ teaspoon cinnamon
½ teaspoon allspice
1 teaspoon ground ginger
Zest of one orange
¼ cup or so pumpkin seeds for top (optional)

Preheat your oven to 350 degrees F.

Sift the flour, salt, sugar, and baking soda together. Add walnuts and candied ginger to your dry ingredients and coat them well. This will keep them suspended in the muffin batter during baking. Set the dry ingredients aside while you mix the wet ingredients.

Mix the pumpkin, oil, eggs, water, spices and orange zest together.

Add the dry ingredients to your wet ingredients and mix them just until they're combined.

Pour the batter into a well-buttered muffin pan. Bake the muffins for 30 minutes, or until a toothpick poked in the very center comes out clean.

Spice Glaze

1 cup powdered sugar
1 teaspoon pure vanilla extract
1 to 2 tablespoons orange juice
½ teaspoon ground cinnamon

Mix the ingredients together. If your glaze is still dry, add a little more orange juice until it can be easily drizzled over the muffins.. Remember you can always add juice, but you can't take it away, so add just a little bit at a time. Allow the muffins to stand for a couple of minutes and then drizzle the glaze over top. It looks so pretty once set, particularly with the pumpkin seeds on top.

Pumpkin Chip Scones

Makes 8 to 10 round scones

The first time I shared this scone recipe was during a cooking class with some of my boys' college friends. The "Camels" (students from Campbell University) arrived ready and willing to participate in some good ol' quality time in the kitchen. Twenty-something students gathered in our kitchen to learn how to make Herb Biscuits, Creamy Potato Leek Soup, and these delicious scones!

2 cups unbleached all-purpose flour
1/3 cup light brown sugar
1 teaspoon ground ginger
½ teaspoon ground cinnamon
½ teaspoon freshly ground nutmeg (fresh is always best when using nutmeg)
½ teaspoon ground mace
2 tablespoons chopped crystallized ginger, optional
1 teaspoon baking powder
½ teaspoon baking soda
¼ teaspoon kosher salt
½ cup salted butter, cut into pieces
1/3 cup semi-sweet or milk chocolate chips

1/3 - ½ cup heavy cream or buttermilk
½ cup canned pure pumpkin (not pie filling)
1 teaspoon pure vanilla extract
1 egg
1 tablespoon cream
Raw sugar for top of scones

Preheat the oven to 400 degrees F and place a rack in the center. Line a baking sheet with parchment paper.

In a large bowl, whisk together the flour, sugar, spices, baking powder, baking soda and salt. Cut the butter into small pieces and blend it into the flour mixture with a pastry blender, two knives or my favorite kitchen the food processor! The mixture should look like coarse crumbs. (If using a food processor place the coarse mixture into a large mixing bowl.) Stir in the ginger and chocolate chips.

In a separate bowl, mix together the buttermilk, pumpkin puree and vanilla and then add the buttermilk mixture to the flour mixture. Mix just until the dough comes together. Do not overmix.

Transfer the dough to a lightly-floured surface. Knead it gently four or five times and then pat the dough into a circle that is about 7 inches round and about 1½ inches thick. You can cut your scones with a biscuit cutter or in the traditional way by cutting the circle in half, then cutting each half into 4 pie-shaped wedges.

In a small bowl, whisk the egg and cream together. This is your egg wash.

Place the scones on your baking sheet. Brush the tops of the scones with the egg wash and sprinkle them with raw sugar.

Place the scones in the middle of the oven. Bake the scones for about 20 minutes or until they're golden brown and a toothpick inserted in the middle comes out clean. Transfer the scones to a wire rack to cool.

Peanut Butter Banana Muffin Tops

Makes 12 muffin tops

1¾ cups unbleached all-purpose flour
1/3 cup light brown sugar
2 teaspoons aluminum-free baking powder
½ teaspoon kosher salt
2 ripe bananas, diced
1 cup half-and-half
1 tablespoon apple cider vinegar
5 1/3 tablespoons salted butter, melted
1/3 cup crunchy peanut butter (We use Smart Balance)
A handful of semi-sweet chocolate chips

Preheat the oven to 375 degrees F. Grease muffin top pans.

In a mixing bowl, combine the flour, brown sugar, baking powder and salt. Add in the diced banana, and stir just a bit.

In a measuring bowl combine the half-and-half and vinegar. Once the half-and-half has curdled just a bit, add in the melted butter and peanut butter and mix them well.

Add the wet ingredients into the dry, stirring only until they're lightly combined. Spoon the muffin batter into each muffin top pan--about 1/3 cup or so for each muffin top. Take care that—once they're all poured--each muffin top has approximately the same amount of batter in it so that they all cook evenly. Top off with a few chocolate chips on top.

Bake the muffin tops for 15 minutes until a toothpick inserted in the center comes out clean. Get your coffee or tea ready, choose your favorite plates, call the family around the table and enjoy! I must admit that everyone in my family ate two, so I hope my own "muffin top" doesn't grow a bit!

Berry Parfaits

Neufchatel cheese is a soft unripened cheese that originated in France. Our American version, which is similar to cream cheese, is made from pasteurized milk and cream and is slightly lower in calories than cream cheese. Regular cream cheese can be substituted for Neufchatel cheese, especially in recipes for dips and spreads, with good results.

This parfait is easy to prepare and feel good about, and its flavors are light and lovely. Who doesn't love a glass dish filled with pretty layers of fresh berries and creamy goodness?

Serves seven hungry people

2 (8-ounce) packages Neufchatel cheese
1 tablespoon pure vanilla extract
½ cup agave nectar
3 tablespoons or more of milk
1 teaspoon ground cinnamon
1½ cups heavy cream
½ cup granulated sugar
1 teaspoon pure almond extract
1 quart strawberries, sliced
1 pint blueberries
1 pint raspberries
1 pint strawberries, hulled and sliced
1 cup red grapes, sliced
1 cup of your favorite granola
Mint leaves for pretty garnish, optional

In a blender whip up your Neufchatel cheese, vanilla extract, agave nectar, milk and cinnamon until they're smooth. You may need to add a bit more milk to get the mixture smooth.

In another bowl, whip your heavy whipping cream, sugar and almond extract for about three to four minutes, or until you achieve a whipped cream consistency.

To make your parfait filling, fold your whipping cream into your Neufchatel cheese mixture.

Place two tablespoons of granola at the bottom of pretty serving glasses or bowls. Next, place a little parfait filling in the glass, followed by a few of the assorted berries, then more parfait filling. Continue this pattern until you reach the top. End with a dollop of whipped cream, a couple of berries, a sprinkling of granola and a small cluster of mint leaves!

A Night of Nostalgia

Back-in-the-Day Salad Wedge with Thousand Island Dressing

Baked Cheeseburger Macaroni and Cheese, Please!

Stuffed Cabbage Rolls or the Lazy Man's Casserole

Old Faithful Whipped Mashed Potatoes

Creamed Corn

My Mom's Baked Pork Chops

Creamy Peanut Butter Milkshakes

Heavenly Chocolate Pudding

Drive-Ins, Rock and Roll music, soda shops, bobbie socks, saddle shoes, poodle skirts and hourglass dresses all hearken back to the good ole days of the 1950s. Although I didn't actually grow up in the 1950s, I do have fond memories of watching Happy Days and Laverne and Shirley in the comfort of my cozy childhood living room in the 1980s with my parents and sister.

Today I take pleasure in listening to the fun music of the 1950s. So when our family decided to help a young boy in need of a handicapped accessible van, a Sock Hop was a natural choice.

My dear friend and her sister made the most charming poodle skirts for us. My friend's skirt was made from a stunning Tartan fabric adorned with the most adorable white Scottish terrier at the bottom. My poodle skirt was a pretty bubblegum pink color, and had a black poodle on the bottom corner that looked very much like my beloved childhood dog, Mademoiselle. The poodle was made from an embossed, fuzzy fabric that felt just like real poodle hair. I tied my hair up in a pony tail with a pink ribbon, and my friend and I wore matching black cardigan sweaters. To add some authenticity to my costume, I chewed on a large piece of pink bubblegum throughout the evening.

Many guests arrived in support of this young boy. A local Classic Car Club set up all of their beautiful shiny antique cars out front of the church building. One week prior to the event, our family spent an afternoon creating a gigantic sign with huge letters that spelled out "Starlite Drive In" to hang on one of the larger church walls. Dozens of chairs were set up under the sign, and a popcorn machine donated by a large rental company added a nostalgic (and fragrant!) touch. Our friends also helped us create an old-fashioned soda shop, which was decorated in pink and silver. A large ice cream shake made out of pink paper and balloons was hung on the wall beside the soda shop. White balloons made up the ice cream, and a red balloon sat on top like a cherry. A straw was made from a tube of shiny red wrapping paper.

Everyone enjoyed the old-fashioned burgers, fries and milk shakes generously donated by Grill 57, a local 1950s style burger joint. Not only did everyone have a fantastic time, but enough money was raised to buy the young man the handicapped accessible van he so desperately needed.

You know, I still have that poodle skirt. It's such a shame to let such a pretty garment sit in my closet. I think I'll get it out and whip up this 1950s inspired menu! I bet my hubby would enjoy coming home to that surprise!

Back-in-the-Day Wedge Salad with Thousand Island Dressing

1 head iceberg lettuce, cut into quarters, washed and dried
½ cup mayonnaise
2 tablespoons chili sauce
1 tablespoon white vinegar
2 teaspoons granulated sugar
1 tablespoon sweet pickle relish
1 tablespoon finely minced white onion
1/8 teaspoon salt
A few grindings black pepper, to taste

Combine the mayonnaise, chili sauce, white vinegar, sugar, relish, onion, salt and pepper in a bowl. Stir them together well. Refrigerate for several hours.

Place a quarter of the iceberg lettuce onto a salad plate and adorn it with your yummy, tangy thousand island dressing!

Baked Cheeseburger Macaroni, Please!

Throw away those boxes of macaroni and cheese! I've got a recipe that is sure to become one of your family's favorites! Various types of pasta can be used for this recipe.

1 pound dried elbow macaroni
1 tablespoon canola oil
1 pound lean ground beef
1 yellow onion, chopped
3 cloves garlic, minced

2 teaspoons kosher salt
1 teaspoon ground black pepper
1 tablespoon plus
1/3 cup butter
1/3 cup unbleached all-purpose flour
3 cups milk
½ teaspoon freshly ground nutmeg
1 teaspoon ground mustard
Pinch of cayenne pepper, optional
4 cups grated mild cheddar cheese
½ cup bread crumbs
1 tablespoon softened butter

In a large pot of salted water, cook your macaroni for 9 to 10 minutes or until it's as tender as you like it. I have substituted whole wheat and multigrain pastas from time to time in this recipe and they are delicious! Drain the cooked pasta and set it aside. You can add a bit of oil so the pasta does not stick.

In a sauté pan, brown the beef, onion and garlic in oil and season with salt and black pepper.

Preheat your oven to 350 degrees F. Coat your 9 x 13-inch baking pan with one tablespoon of softened butter.

In a large saucepan, melt the butter over medium heat. Stir the flour into the butter until it's smooth. Slowly add in the milk and continue stirring until the mixture thickens. Add in the ground nutmeg, dry mustard and cayenne pepper and stir together well. Stir in the cheddar--a small handful at a time--until cheese is fully incorporated. Add in the ground beef mixture and the cooked pasta and mix well.

Pour the pasta into a prepared baking dish.

Spread breadcrumbs over top of the pasta. Bake it uncovered for 45 minutes, or until it bubbles around the edges. Sometimes, when I have it on hand, I will spray the breadcrumbs with a little butter spray.

Golabki (Stuffed Cabbage Rolls)

When I was a little girl, the Polish Club in Fall River, Massachusetts made the best stuffed cabbage rolls and pierogies. On occasion my mom would call my dad and ask him to stop and pick up stuffed cabbage rolls on his way home from work. I remember sitting on our long cozy window seat, anxiously waiting for his car to pull up in front of the house. (When telling a good friend this story once, she commented "Most girls wait by the window in anticipation of their first date, but you . . . you waited by the window in anticipation of food!" She's right. I'll never be thin!)

As my father's vehicle approached I'd exclaim "Here comes Dad!" A minute later I'd hear the downstairs door open and close and my father's footsteps ascending up the stairs past my grandmother's apartment. As soon as our apartment door opened, the aroma of mouth-watering cabbage rolls filled the air. With forks in hand and a bottle of ketchup on the table, Mom and I were ready to dive in!

A couple of decades later, my parents came to visit us in upstate New York. I was newly married and I wanted to surprise them. I created a recipe that tasted just like the cabbage rolls I grew up devouring. I was certain that this thoughtful dinner would bring back joyful memories. Upon entering our townhouse, my mom's face lit up as she recognized the familiar smell. Dad didn't say much, but he was always somewhat of a quiet man, and I didn't give his silence a second thought.

Later that evening, as we sat around the table eating our dinner, I noticed that my dad was eating very slowly, and had not said much about the cabbage rolls.

I asked him if anything was the matter, and he replied, "This dinner was so thoughtful of you, but I have always hated cabbage rolls. I would buy the cabbage rolls for you and mom and pierogies for myself!" I was so embarrassed! But my dad sat there and lovingly ate every bite. What a guy!

1 large head of green cabbage
½ pound ground beef, uncooked
½ pound ground pork, uncooked
2 large eggs
1 large onion, grated (use the juice, too)
1 tablespoon Worcestershire sauce
1 teaspoon kosher salt
1 tablespoon ketchup
½ teaspoon ground black pepper
3 cups cooked rice, cooled
½ cup ketchup or chili sauce for the top of the rolls

Cut a deep X in the core of your cabbage. Place the cabbage in a large pot of boiling water. Keep checking on the leaves and use your tongs to separate them as they loosen. Remove onto a plate and continue cooking the rest of the cabbage until all leaves have been separated.

In a bowl combine the uncooked ground beef, pork, eggs, grated onion and its juices, Worcestershire sauce, salt, pepper, ketchup and cooked cool rice. Divide mixture between cabbage leaves, placing some in the middle of each leaf. Tuck the sides of each cabbage leaf in and roll them up. Line a 9 x 13-inch baking pan with extra cabbage leaves. Place rolls seam side down and brush a little ketchup or chili sauce on top. Cover the cabbage rolls and bake them in a 350 degree F oven for 1 hour. Serve the rolls with mashed potatoes.

Here's a great tip for you! If you have a hankering for Stuffed Cabbage Rolls, but you have no time to roll them (or you are just plain feeling lazy), no problem, thanks to my uncle George. This is an easy way to serve up the same flavors, but with a little less time:

Place two layers of your blanched cabbage leaves on the bottom of a 9 x 13-inch baking pan. Spread your meat and rice filling over the cabbage. Add two more layers of cabbage and a good brushing of ketchup or chili sauce. Bake the dish in the oven for the same amount of time as the recipe suggests. Let cool slightly, then cut just like lasagna. I could have kissed Uncle George when he suggested this, but I was in North Carolina and he was in Massachusetts at the time!

Old Faithful Whipped Mashed Potatoes

3 pounds russet potatoes, peeled
3 garlic cloves, smashed
1stick salted butter
1 cup milk
Kosher Salt and Pepper, to taste

Place the potatoes and garlic cloves in a large pan and cover them with cold water. To ensure even cooking, potatoes should be cut in uniform sizes and always started in cold water.

While your potatoes cook, heat up the milk and butter. Cook the potatoes just until fork tender. Overcooking your potatoes will make them gummy. Drain the potatoes well and place them in an electric mixing bowl or a regular bowl.

When I was a child, my mother and I would use her hand mixer, but today I use my standing mixer's to whip up my potatoes. Add in your milk/butter mixture, along with salt and pepper. Then whip, whip, whip those potatoes until you achieve the consistency you like. Always taste to see if more salt or pepper should be added.

Creamed Corn

2 tablespoons butter
½ yellow onion, diced
1 garlic clove, minced
2 tablespoons flour
1 ½ pounds frozen corn
1 cup heavy or whipping cream
½ teaspoon freshly ground nutmeg
1 teaspoon kosher salt (or salt to taste)
½ teaspoon freshly ground black pepper
Garnish with freshly chopped parsley

In a sauté pan, melt the butter and then add in the diced onion. Sauté the onion for two to three minutes or until it's translucent. Do not brown the onion.

Add in the garlic and cook it for one minute. Add in the flour and cook the mixture for a minute or so to remove the flour taste. Add in your corn and cream. Season with salt, pepper and freshly ground nutmeg. Cook the mixture just until the cream thickens a bit. The cream will continue to set up as it sits, so keeping it a little loose is a good idea.

Garnish the creamed corn with freshly chopped parsley, chives or scallions and enjoy!

Mom's Baked Pork Chops

Serves 4 to 6 people

    I remember my mother making this recipe often during my childhood. Whether I was in my room doing homework, coming in after playing sports with friends, or just coming back from a run with my dad, the meaty, savory scent of these pork chops filling the house would make me so hungry that it was difficult to wait for dinner! Mom always served these crispy, flavorful pork chops with mashed potatoes and corn. I love making these for my family! They are actually very lean and low in fat because you do not use oil or butter. Using fresh red crushed pepper is much better than a sprinkling of dried crushed pepper.

4 to 6 pork chops with the bone in
¼ teaspoon fresh Pimento moida, a fresh Portuguese red crushed pepper on each side
Garlic powder
Onion powder

Preheat your oven to 375 degrees F.

Place the pork chops in your broiler pan. Simply rub a little (about ¼ teaspoon) Pimento Moida or fresh red crushed pepper over each side of your chops and sprinkle each one with a good amount of garlic and onion powder. Do not touch your eyes and wash your hands right away after handling the Pimento Moida, as it's a very hot, spicy mixture. My mom liked to bake the pork chops in a 350 degree oven until they were crispy, but not dry. The cook time will depend on the thickness of your chops. Pork chops should be cooked to the internal temperature of 145 degrees F.

Peanut Butter Milkshakes

As a child I loved getting together with family and friends on the weekends. I liked being busy so I would too often ask my parents "What are we doing today? Are we going swimming at Aunt Alice's or Aunt Rosie's? Can we all go to the park and ride our bikes? Can we to spend the day at the beach with the Valencias?"

The Valencias were our neighbors a few doors down. Their son Ralph and I were good friends. My sister, April, was good friends with Ralph's sister, Melissa, and so our families would often get together for trips to the beach and for cookouts. You don't need a lot of money to spend quality time as a family.

When I was a child, every now and then Dad or Mom would call out, "We're going on a mystery ride!" and my sister and I would squeal and make our way to the front door. The fun of not knowing where we'd end up on these rides was always just as good as the destination!

Sometimes the destination was a little ice cream shop on route 66 in Westport, Massachusetts. Everyone in our family loves ice cream—especially me! The shop had a swing set on the side. We would all enjoy our ice cream and then Mom and Dad would push us on the swings. Dad would sometimes push mom on the swings, too. That was always so sweet.

Decades later during one of my parents' summer visits to our home in Asheville, North Carolina, we indulged our long-time love of ice cream by making different types of thick and creamy milkshakes. After my parents returned home they sent us the pretty, old-fashioned green milkshake maker that once sat in a corner of their kitchen.

We love milkshakes and have put mom and dad's blender to good use! Peanut butter is our family's personal favorite, but you can substitute the peanut butter with chocolate fudge or frozen or fresh fruit.

1 cup milk
2 cups vanilla ice cream
¾ cup creamy peanut butter
1 tablespoon pure vanilla extract

This recipe is super-easy! Simply combine all of the ingredients in a blender and blend them until nice and smooth. Pour the shakes into your favorite glasses and enjoy!

Heavenly Chocolate Pudding

On certain afternoons, I would smile and ask my grandmother, "Vavo, did you happen to make pudding today?" Her reply was almost always, "*Of course, it's in the refrigerator!*" I would run to the refrigerator, where Vavo's pretty pudding glasses, each a different size and each decorated with different edges or etchings, would be filled with chocolate, vanilla, butterscotch or pistachio pudding.

After our house fire in 2000, my mother gave my grandmother's treasured pudding glasses to me. Oh, the memories! I still love stovetop puddings. My favorite part has always been the skin that forms on top as the pudding cools. Today my husband, children and I enjoy these beautiful glasses and the homemade puddings in them – just as I had done as a child!

½ cup granulated sugar

3 tablespoons good unsweetened cocoa powder

¼ cup cornstarch

1/8 teaspoon salt

2¾ cup milk

2 tablespoons butter

1 teaspoon pure vanilla extract

½ teaspoon almond extract, optional

In a large saucepan, stir together the sugar, cocoa powder, cornstarch, salt and milk. Bring it to a full boil, stirring constantly. Let this silky chocolate creation thicken until it coats the back of a metal spoon. Remove the pudding from the heat and stir in the butter and vanilla. Pour this decadent mixture into your pudding cups and refrigerate until it sets completely.

Speaking of chocolate pudding, I just have to share this adorable story written by my dear Amanda Michelle Creech...

"*Get Me a Man* Pie"

When it comes to cooking, Elise and my family say my thing is cupcakes. I love to experiment with flavors and decorations, but if I want to make a dessert that will really impress, hands down, I make Get Me a Man Pie. This pie started out with a much more humble name, the name by which I still call it, Granny's Chocolate Pie. You see, this decadent pie comes from a recipe that my great-grandmother used to make every year for her middle daughter's—my grandmother's--birthday.

I was twelve and just starting to get interested in baking when my Granny passed away, just days before my grandma's birthday. I decided that my grandma could not lose the cherished tradition of having Granny's chocolate pie, so I must carry on the custom. For ten years I have made the pie for grandma's birthday, but last Valentine's Day I made it for another reason.

Elise's oldest son Nate and I had known each other for several months and had started spending more time together. I had begun to think that I might be interested in him as more than a friend, so I more than gladly accepted his invitation to go to dinner with him and watch Casablanca on Valentine's Day.

Of course, I wanted to impress Nate so I decided to make the one dessert that I was sure would do the trick. That's right; I made Granny's chocolate pie. In talking with my mom before the date, I jokingly told her that I was turning the pie into my "get me a man pie" in hopes that Nate would find my dessert-making skills impressive. My mom thought the name was hilarious and before I knew it, it stuck. Nate loved the pie and asks me to make it regularly.

I guess the pie worked because over a year later, Nate and I are still together. Once again, we went to dinner and watched Casablanca for Valentine's Day, and of course I made our *"Got Me a Man* Pie."

BIRTHDAY BASHES

GRILLIN', CHILLIN' AND CELEBRATIN'!

Grilled Spinach Turkey Feta Burgers with Green Goddess Mayo

Grilled Lemon Chicken

Tortellini Salad

Party Beans

Summer Potato Salad

Hawaiian Cake

Pecan Bars

Written by my son, Nathaniel

Birthdays are special days, and because of that, birthday memories have a funny way of staying around in your mind. Because my birthday falls in the month of July, right in the heat of the summer, for most of my 22 years on this Earth my parties have typically been built around a favorite theme of mine--a summer barbecue. Whether we had our birthday barbecue celebration at home, a local park, or a nearby lake, we always participated in the same fun activities: bonfires, water gun fights, outdoor games, and even the occasional launching of some fireworks left over from the 4th of July.

While I enjoyed all of those things, they were never the most amazing part of my birthday. One thing was always memorable and more brilliant than everything else—the food. There was nothing else on that day that inspired more compliments, more fun, or more memories than the delicious spread laid out on our family table. My favorite summer dishes always included at my parties were hot-dogs, baked beans, a cool summer salad, homemade burgers, and my personal favorite--tortellini pasta salad. Of course, to top everything off, there was always a homemade cake made by mom with ice cream on the side.

One of my favorite aspects of the food served at those parties is that each dish doesn't just bring to mind birthday memories, but special highlights throughout the years. A bite of salad reminds me of my 14th birthday, when we celebrated around a campfire the year our family moved to a new house that sat beside a lake. A bite of hamburger takes me back to the massive water gun fight we had on my 12th birthday and the amazing baseball season I had that year when I played my personal best. The pasta salad always makes me remember my 16th birthday party where it seemed like the whole neighborhood turned out to celebrate. It also reminds me of my favorite days sailing on the water for hours on end.

For me, food does so much more than nourish my body. It reminds me of the best days of the past, and makes me excited about creating memories in the future.

Spinach Feta Turkey Burgers with Green Goddess Mayo

Turkey Burgers

Serves 4

1 ½ pounds lean ground turkey
1 cup frozen spinach, thawed, drained and finely chopped
2 large egg yolks
½ cup reduced fat feta cheese
2 teaspoons kosher salt
¼ teaspoon cayenne pepper
2 teaspoons garlic powder
1 tablespoon onion powder
Green Goddess Dressing (below)
Tomato slices and lettuce leaves for garnish

In a large bowl, mix together the ground turkey, spinach, egg yolks, feta cheese, salt, cayenne pepper and garlic and onion powder. Divide the meat into equal amounts and form patties. Place each burger between waxed paper and store the burgers in the refrigerator until you are ready to grill them.

Green Goddess Mayonnaise

½ cup mayonnaise
½ cup sour cream
Juice of half of a lemon
Salt and pepper to taste
Handful of cilantro

In a blender, blend together the mayonnaise, sour cream, lemon juice, salt, pepper and cilantro.

Cook your burgers on the grill or in a skillet with a little vegetable oil for about 6 or 7 minutes per side. Serve them on your favorite hamburger bun slathered with Green Goddess Dressing, a fresh slice of tomato and crispy lettuce leaves.

Grilled Lemon Chicken

I love marinating meats and poultry, particularly when I'm preparing for a party. When marinating food in plastic storage bags in the refrigerator, always store the bag on a plate or in a bowl. If the bag should leak, you've saved yourself a lot of clean-up time!

4 chicken breasts (boneless or bone-in)
¼ cup olive oil
Zest and juice of one large lemon
1 teaspoon low-sodium soy sauce
1 teaspoon finely chopped fresh rosemary
1 teaspoon finely chopped fresh thyme
3 cloves garlic, minced
1 shallot, finely chopped
1/8 teaspoon cayenne pepper
1 teaspoon kosher salt
½ teaspoon white pepper
2 lemons, thickly sliced

Combine the chicken breasts, olive oil, lemon juice, lemon zest, soy sauce, rosemary, thyme, garlic, shallot, cayenne, salt and pepper in a plastic storage bag. Let the chicken marinate overnight, or for at least four hours.

Cook the lemon slices on the grill just for a few seconds and set them aside. Grill your chicken until the juices run clear. The time this will take will depend on the size of your chicken pieces and whether they are bone-in or boneless. Boneless chicken cooks a bit faster than bone-in chicken. Chicken should be cooked to an internal temperature of 165 degrees F.

Arrange the chicken breasts on a platter. Decorate with fresh sprigs of rosemary and thyme and the pretty grilled lemon slices. Enjoy!

Tortellini Salad

20 ounces fresh or frozen cheese tortellini
2 cups cubed pepperoni, chopped
1 (14.5-ounce) can small black olives, drained (kalamata olives are good, too)
2 jars artichokes in oil or water, drained
1 cup freshly grated Parmesan cheese
½ green bell pepper, chopped
½ red bell pepper, chopped
1 bunch chives, chopped
1 pint cherry tomatoes, halved
1 (8-ounce) block mozzarella cheese, cut into bite size cubes
½ cup chopped parsley
12 ounces Italian dressing – the zestier the better
Zest of 1 lemon

Boil the tortellini for five minutes or until they pop up to the top of the water. Drain the pasta and combine it with all of the other ingredients in a large bowl. Cover the pasta and refrigerate it overnight, or for at least four hours.

Party Beans

½ pound bacon, chopped
½ yellow onion, chopped
½ green bell pepper, chopped
3 cloves garlic, minced
1 (15-ounce) can navy beans
1 (15-ounce can) black beans
1 (15-ounce) can red kidney beans
½ cup chili sauce or ketchup
2 tablespoon Worcestershire sauce
4 tablespoon molasses, brown sugar, maple syrup or honey
1 tablespoon yellow or Dijon mustard

In a skillet, cook the bacon until it's nice and crispy. Remove the bacon from the pan and set it aside.

In the same pan, cook the onion, green pepper and garlic in the bacon fat until it's almost tender.

Mix all of the ingredients in a 9 x 13-inch pan. Bake the beans uncovered in a 350-degree F oven for one hour.

Summer Potato Salad

This tangy side dish is perfect for hot summer months. This potato salad can be kept out in the heat for a longer period than potato salad recipes that call for mayonnaise.

8 large russet potatoes
½ pound bacon, chopped
2 yellow onions, chopped
2 cloves of garlic, minced
2 tablespoons all-purpose unbleached flour
2 tablespoons granulated sugar
2 teaspoons kosher salt
½ teaspoon ground black pepper
¾ cup water
1½ cups malt vinegar (if you can get a German brand of vinegar it will be even better)
Two tablespoons chopped chives

Boil your potatoes in lightly salted water until tender, but still firm. If you over-boil them you will end up with mush.

While your potatoes are bubbling away, cook your bacon in a sauté pan until it's browned and crispy. Remove the bacon and reserve it on a plate for later.

Add in the onions and garlic and cook them until they're tender. Stir in the flour, sugar and salt and vinegar into your sauté pan. Let the mixture thicken for one minute or so.

Pour the vinegar mixture over your potatoes. Gently stir and garnish with chopped chives and crispy bacon. Serve warm or at room temperature.

Hawaiian Cake

Cake

2 cups unbleached all purpose flour
2 cups granulated sugar
1 teaspoon aluminum-free baking powder
½ teaspoon baking soda
1 cup almond slivers, optional
1 cup flaked coconut
2 large eggs, beaten
½ cup canola or coconut oil
1 (20-ounce) can crushed pineapple in juice (include the juice)

Frosting

1 (8-ounce) container cream cheese with pineapple
½ cup butter, softened
½ teaspoon pure vanilla extract
1 teaspoon pure almond extract
1 cup powdered or confectioners' sugar
½ cup toasted almonds
½ cup toasted coconut

Preheat your oven to 350 degrees F. Grease and flour a 9 x 13-inch baking pan.

In a large mixing bowl, combine the flour, granulated sugar, baking powder and soda, coconut and pecans. In another bowl beat together the eggs, oil, pineapple and pineapple juice. Combine wet and dry ingredients.

Pour the batter into your prepared pan. Bake the cake for 35 to 40 minutes, or until a toothpick inserted in the center comes out clean. Let the cake cool on a wire rack.

While your cake bakes, prepare the frosting by blending the cream cheese, butter, vanilla and almond extracts and powdered sugar. Spread the frosting topping over the cake while it's still warm.

Pecan Bars

Makes 3 dozen

I like serving both a birthday cake and one other dessert at birthday parties. These nut bars are similar to mini pecan pies, and are just as gooey and addicting. Don't say I didn't warn you!

Crust

1 tablespoon plus ¾ cup cold butter, divided
2 1/3 cups unbleached all-purpose flour
½ cup granulated sugar
½ teaspoon baking powder
½ teaspoon kosher salt
1 large egg, lightly beaten

Topping

2/3 cup raw honey
½ cup packed light brown sugar
¼ teaspoon kosher salt
6 tablespoons cold butter, cubed
2 tablespoons heavy whipping cream
4 cups whole pecans or other nut

Line a 9 x 13-inch baking pan with 1 tablespoon of softened butter. This is a very important step--you'll thank me when you remove the bars from your pan later!

In a large bowl, combine the flour, sugar, baking powder, and salt. Cut in the remaining butter and mix it until it resembles coarse crumbs. Stir in the egg until it's blended in. The mixture will be dry—press it firmly into prepared pan.

Bake the crust in a 375 degree F oven for 18 to 20 minutes or until the edges are golden brown. Cool on a wire rack.

Meanwhile, in a large, heavy saucepan, bring the honey, brown sugar, and salt to a boil over medium heat. This is your caramel base. Stir the mixture until the sugar is dissolved, then boil it without stirring for two minutes. Add in the butter and cream. Bring the mixture back up to a boil and cook and stir it for 1 minute. Be sure not to overcook your caramel. You, your family and your friends will end up in the dentist's office - I know from experience! I once cooked the caramel too long, brought my beautiful bars to a dessert party and watched in horror as everyone tried to eat them–so learn from my mistake! Remove the sauce from the heat and stir in the nuts. Spread the caramel and nut mixture over the crust.

Bake the bars at 375 degrees F for 15 to 20 minutes more or until the topping is bubbly. Cool the bars completely on a wire rack. This will ensure that they come out of the pan easily!

Once they're cooled, slide the pecan bars out of the pan and cut them into pieces.

TIP: If you have parchment paper on hand, you can line your baking pan with it adding a little extra for pulling up out of the pan later. The parchment paper makes clean up much easier, too. Nothin' bad about that!

Whenever I think of pecan pie or pecan bars Kim Colley's witty and heartwarming story about her Mamma's Pecan Pie brings a smile to my face and joy to my heart...

"Mamma's Pecan Pie" by Kim Colley

In memory of Bernice Wooten

My favorite holiday memories are those that involve going home to Grandma's house. I know it sounds a little cliché, but it's the truth. However, we didn't call her grandma; she was "Mamma."

Mamma was the twelfth of fifteen children. She married a minister and then immediately put all of the many recipes she'd acquired over the years into practice. Mamma didn't just cook for her family, but for the church family, which included visiting ministers and their families.

When I became the woman of my own home, there was only one woman to call; Mamma. I knew she could supply me with the best recipes for my new family and any guests I might have. I'll never forget the first time I called her for help. I was determined to make my Southern husband the best pecan pie. When she answered the phone, I immediately felt like I'd tapped into the "bat signal". Help was on the way! Mamma walked me carefully through each step of how to make "her" pecan pie--the pie she had made so many times before for my Pappa and for the holidays. We even sat on the phone talking while it baked. Before hanging up, I had to promise I would call her later with a taste report.

I wish I could tell you I learned a lesson and wrote the pie recipe down, but I didn't. As the years passed I called Mamma time after time for the pecan pie recipe, along with many others. Finally, I got smart. One Christmas I asked her to write down all her favorite recipes. I requested that she include why they were her favorites and how and where she had obtained them. That Christmas I received a cookbook full of recipes that Mamma had penned by hand. I was so excited!

I'll never forget the moment when I flipped through to the dessert section to the famous pecan pie recipe that I had called her for so many times. She had always taken the time to walk me through the recipe step by step, sit with me while the pie baked, and catch up with my interests and my family, church and friends. The recipe was clear and simple, but I was curious about who had shared it with her. That's when I saw her little note to me at the bottom of the page. It said:

"Psst, If you ever lose this book or this recipe page, the recipe can be found on the back of the Karo Syrup bottle. Love Mamma."

Those words spoke volumes to me. I knew she loved me. She could have told me where the recipe came from a long time ago, but then think of all of the conversations we would have missed!

KLINGON BANQUET

Romulan Ale

Heart of Targ (Sesame Chicken)

Gagh (Noodles in Peanut Sauce)

Generations Cake (Carrot Pineapple Cake)

Written by my son, Alexander

My family and I are enormous fans of Star Trek! I remember that every Wednesday night we would gather in our living room--after having eaten a hearty dinner of course--to watch the latest incarnation of this classic science-fiction series. As young children, my friends, brother and I would frequently dress up as the various alien species and characters from the show and act out scenes from the movies and television shows in a way that only children raised on sci-fi could.

I wanted to take this a step further, so on my ninth birthday, I asked my parents if I could have a Star Trek-themed birthday party. We decided we would not only make it a Star Trek birthday party, but that we'd go the extra mile and throw a Klingon birthday banquet. The Klingons were a popular, albeit barbaric and vulgar species from the show who had a long list of revolting cuisine.

Mom, however, was up to the challenge! Using her recipe for Sesame Chicken, she created the traditional Klingon dish of Heart of Targ as the entrée. She then made a side dish of peanut butter noodles as Gagh--a dish of live worms that Trekkies know is a staple for any Klingon meal.

For drinks, we poured ginger ale into several clear pitchers and mixed in blue dye, creating another Klingon staple, Romulan Ale.

To my dismay, fruit punch was served as a substitute for Klingon Blood Wine which Mom explained would be, "too hard to make." On the night of the party, Dad taped red paper over the lights above the dining room table, casting an eerie red glow over the entire room as mom created Klingon shoulder pauldrons for everyone to wear. The ensuing cacophony was a mix of guttural burps, war chants and fists pounding on the table as we waited expectantly and obnoxiously for our food to arrive in true Klingon fashion.

Growing up, we always had something to look forward to as a family, as we always spent time together and joined in on each other's passions and hobbies. Memories of that night always remind me of how tight-knit my family was and still is. And yes, we still eagerly await the release of each Star Trek movie with geeky gusto!

Romulan Ale

The easiest party drink you'll ever make, this "Romulan Ale" was the perfect start to our Klingon Banquet. This bright blue drink, served in a large, clear glass pitcher and clear glass cups made a fun and unique centerpiece for our banquet table.

Glass pitcher and clear goblets or glasses
1 (2-liter) bottle ginger ale
Several drops of blue food coloring

Klingon "Heart of Targ" or Sesame Chicken

4 chicken breasts, rinsed, patted dry with paper towels and cut into 2-inch pieces
¾ cup unbleached all-purpose flour
1 teaspoon kosher salt
½ teaspoon ground black pepper
1 teaspoon garlic powder
½ teaspoon ground ginger
2 extra large eggs, lightly beaten
1 cup sesame seeds
Vegetable oil for pan frying

Combine flour, salt, pepper, garlic powder and ginger on a plate. Dredge your chicken pieces in flour, then in the egg, then flour again, then egg again, then finish them off with a coating of sesame seeds.

Heat your skillet with a little canola or vegetable oil and brown all sides of your chicken until it is cooked through. To preserve moisture, don't cook your chicken past an internal temperature of 165 degrees F.

Klingon "Gagh" or Noodles in Peanut Sauce

2 teaspoons dark sesame oil
4 cloves garlic, minced
6 scallions, chopped
4 tablespoons light soy sauce
2 teaspoons ground ginger
½ teaspoon dried red pepper flakes
1 cup creamy peanut butter (the less sugar in the peanut butter the better)
2 cup low-sodium chicken broth
1 pound spaghetti, cooked

In a medium saucepan, heat the sesame oil and add in the garlic and scallions and cook for one minute. Add in the soy sauce, ginger, red pepper flakes and peanut butter.

Stir the mixture for one minute more, and then add in the chicken broth. Cook the mixture for 5 minutes, or until it's smooth. Coat your cooked noodles with peanut sauce, reserving some for dipping your Sesame Chicken.

With a name like Generations Cake, this was the perfect cake for a Star Trek-inspired birthday cake!

The Generations Cake

My children are what we call third generation Trekkies. I watched Star Trek with my father as a child. My husband's mother (Nana to the boys) is a huge Star Trek fan and so she and Mike often watched Star Trek together. Mike and I have watched every Star Trek episode and movie (dare I say more than once) with our boys.

"Star Trek: The Next Generation" is my husband's favorite series. Nate and I enjoyed "Voyager" the most. Alexander and Nana's favorite is without a doubt "Deep Space Nine."

This carrot pineapple cake, loved by all three generations, has found its place on our family table for special occasions like birthdays. Because all three generations love it we call it "The Generations Cake." With a name like Generations, it was the perfect choice for a Star Trek birthday party.

Cake

2 cups unbleached all-purpose flour
2 teaspoons ground cinnamon
1 teaspoon ground ginger
½ teaspoon ground cloves
½ teaspoon freshly ground nutmeg
1½ teaspoons baking soda
2 teaspoons baking powder
1 teaspoon kosher salt
2 cups grated carrots
2 cups granulated sugar
4 large eggs
1½ cups vegetable oil
1 teaspoon pure vanilla extract
1 (8-ounce) can crushed pineapple and its juices
1 cup chopped walnuts, optional
1/4 cup candied ginger

Cream Cheese Frosting

2 (8-ounce) packages cream cheese, softened
½ cup softened butter
1 teaspoon pure vanilla extract
Powdered sugar

Mix all of the ingredients together, adding enough powdered sugar to make the frosting thick. Set the frosting aside.

Sift the dry ingredients and walnuts together in a bowl. In a mixer, combine the sugar, eggs, oil and vanilla. Add the dry ingredients into the wet ingredients and mix them together well. Fold in the pineapple. Pour the batter into two 8-inch round cake pans sprayed with non-stick cooking spray. Bake the in a 350-degree F oven until a toothpick inserted in the center comes out clean-- about 45 to 50 minutes. Allow the cake to cool on a wire rack. You can use this batter to make cupcakes, round cakes or rectangular cakes. The cooking time will be much less for cupcakes. However you make it, frost it generously with Cream Cheese Frosting.

This Klingon Banquet was one of the most memorable of Alex's birthdays!

When thinking about cakes enjoyed by several generations, I am reminded of this priceless story…

Another special generation's cake -- "Granny's Pineapple Cake"

Written by our dear Amanda Michelle Creech in loving memory of her Granny, Della Gladys Lee

It was a typical Sunday morning in November. I was twelve years old. I was getting ready for church when the phone rang. It was very unusual for anyone to call my family on a Sunday morning, so I went into my parents' room to see who it could be. My mom was sitting on her bed crying her eyes out, and I knew something was terribly wrong. Through her tears, she fought out two simple words that still haunt me. "Granny's dead," she sobbed. Stunned, I said nothing. I simply walked back into my room and changed out of my church clothes into jeans and a sweater. I knew that we were no longer going to church, but to Smithfield where "Granny", my great grandmother had lived.

Now, my Granny lived in a tiny two bedroom farm house on land that had been in her husband's family for somewhere around a century. Her two oldest daughters and their husbands lived just down a gravel path, and had both raised their children there. My granny had celebrated her 89th birthday a few weeks before, and other than the aches and minor ailments that afflicted any person her age, was the picture of health. She still worked in the yard at least once a week, drove herself around town with no problems, and had a sharper mind than I do now at the age of twenty-two.

My family arrived at her house to find my grandma—who was Granny's middle daughter--Papa, and several other family members already gathered. We quickly learned that Granny had no signs of sickness or pain the night before. When she didn't call her oldest daughter, my great-aunt, that morning for a ride to church, my aunt became worried. She called my grandmother and they both went with my papa to check on Granny. They found her lying peacefully in her bed with her church clothes hanging on the door. She had apparently slipped away to heaven sometime in the night, with no pain or suffering whatsoever. The most touching part of the whole situation, however, was probably what they found on the kitchen counter.

My granny was the oldest girl of eleven children. Her youngest brother was born a few months after Granny delivered her first child. Granny was like another mother to my Uncle Marvin, and he loved her dearly. (We were told that he threw the phone when they called to tell him of Granny's death). He and his wife were scheduled to visit Granny that Sunday afternoon. On the kitchen counter was a pineapple cake Granny had made for the visit. We debated whether or not to eat the cake out of respect for her, but we quickly decided that Granny would want us to eat it. In exact keeping with her servant's heart, Granny had unknowingly baked for her own funeral! We set aside a piece of cake for Uncle Marvin, of course, and then we each enjoyed a slice. It was without a doubt the best pineapple cake I've ever eaten and probably will ever eat. Granny had baked it with love for her brother, and that love resonated with every bite.

Notes and Memories

PART TWO

No Passport Necessary

INTERNATIONAL CUISINE

Expanding your family's world ... one meal at a time

Our family has always embraced all cultures and cuisines. For many years we organized International Nights for homeschool groups. After finding a large venue where everyone could meet, each participating family chose a country of interest, spent several weeks immersed in exploration and then came up with great exhibits to share with each other. Some people chose to sing, dance, play musical instruments, or read poetry, while others used art or science projects to illustrate the knowledge they had gained. We ourselves had the most fun studying England, China and Greece. I think the best time we ever had was the year we created a display based on our vacation in England.

I really began experimenting with other cuisines when my son Alexander was preparing for the National Geographic Bee in 2006. Helping Alexander study for the Bee was mutually beneficial. I remember the hours we spent together learning map terminology, the interconnectedness of geography (such as physical features, climate, culture and current events.) Our family meal times included quizzing Alexander and enjoying a meal inspired by one of the cultures he was studying that week.

Here, in this second part of the book, we have shared our favorite international recipes with you. Some of these recipes, like the Chicken Tikka Masala, later became winning recipes at cooking competitions in which I participated.

Once you've tried the international recipes provided in this section, we hope you will continue to choose to learn about different countries and cuisines that interest your family. You too can expand your family's world...one meal a time!

PORTUGAL

Portuguese Kale Soup

My Vavo's Pan Fried Fish and Red Gravy with Boiled Stewed Potatoes

Portuguese Stuffing

My Grandmother's Spaghetti and Meatballs

Portuguese Malasadas (Portuguese Fried Doughnuts)

Massa Sovada (Portuguese Sweet Bread)

I would be remiss if I did not begin this portion of my book with recipes from my grandmother's beautiful homeland. The Azores is a cluster of nine volcanic islands situated in the middle of the North Atlantic Ocean, about 930 miles west of Lisbon, Portugal. One of these islands is São Miguel. This is where my ancestors came from.

My grandmother, Mary Isabel Medeiros Duarte, was born in the village of Livremente. At the age of two years old she immigrated to the United States with her mother and father. Unfortunately her mother died shortly afterwards and my grandmother was sent to live with her mother's family in Sao Miguel. We think she was approximately fifteen or sixteen years old when she was called back to the states.

I learned a great deal from my grandmother. I believe we got along so well because we both thought so much alike. During breakfast we'd discuss our plans for lunch and during lunch we'd discuss our plans for dinner!

When I was in high school my parents moved to a townhouse up the road from where I grew up, so we were never far from my grandmother.

When I was older I moved into my own apartment, which was across the street from my grandmother. I spent a great deal of time with her for most of my young life.

My grandmother visited her homeland every year. Before she left on her trips, she collected bags of clothing and much-needed items for the less fortunate living in the Azores. She shipped these bags overseas so that once she arrived she could distribute the items herself. My grandmother loved to fly. She loved visiting the Azores. And she just loved the little house she owned on the island. Her cousins lived there year-round, and Vavo made certain that the house was always cared for.

In the spring of 1990, my grandmother made her yearly trip to Portugal. During her vacation she spent days doing what she loved -- filling people's bellies and hearts. Just before she was scheduled to return home, she hosted one last dinner party. During the dinner, she suddenly felt ill. Towards the end of the evening, she suffered a massive heart attack and died. Her body was flown back to her children and grandchildren in the States and a proper funeral was held for her, but not before the people of the Azores had their chance to say goodbye.

One July, twenty-one years later, while visiting family in New England, I decided it was time to return to my grandmother's home–the home I grew up in as a child. My grandmother had left the house in the States to my uncle George. He has lived in and lovingly cared for the house over the years.

As we walked up to the door I noticed that the tiny strip of thick, green grass behind the aluminum fence was still trimmed to perfection. I walked up the concrete steps and opened the tiny aluminum gate, just as I had done thousands of times as a child. My heart began to beat a little faster, and I found myself fighting back tears.

Walking into the front room of my grandmother's home was like stepping back in time. Everything was exactly how she'd left it. But for the addition of a new sofa, the room where she would sit and enjoy the Lawrence Welk Show and The Golden Girls looked just the same as always.

The formal parlor, which sat at the front of the house, was exactly as I remembered it. A beautiful painting of my grandparents still hung on one wall.

My mother walked me over to the front sunroom where my grandmother did all of her sewing. As she opened the door, I could have sworn that I heard the sound of my Vavo's sewing machine.

I could almost see Vavo sitting right in the corner of the little room, pins in her mouth, making the most beautiful creations as homemade patterns, scissors, her measuring tape and my cat, Midnight, lay on the floor around her. Tucked away in one corner of the room was the fine-looking wooden manger my father had lovingly made for her. My grandmother loved my father as if he was her own and he loved her just the same.

Near the sunroom was the entryway and staircase that led to our former second-floor apartment. This also looked just as I remembered it. My mother had always kept this entry immaculate, carefully washing the stairs and woodwork each week. The bathroom, my uncle's bedroom and my grandmother's bedroom sat nearly untouched. What a blessing to experience every sight and smell, just as I remembered it!

Finally, we made our way down the tiny wooden steps of the little basement. There at the bottom of the stairs was my grandmother's kitchen, looking as though time had passed it by. There were the same wooden cabinets, the old marble-style Formica countertops, and the little window, still dressed in its friendly white checkered curtain. Under my grown-up feet was the same gold and brown vinyl floor I'd walked across so many times as a child. In the center of the little room was the tiny table that my grandmother and I had sat at together to both prepare and enjoy family meals. Through tear-filled eyes, I looked at the metal plate rack sitting in the dry part of the sink. How many times had I helped my grandmother clean up by placing silverware, cups and plates in that rack? The place settings were tucked away in the cabinets like always. One of the cupboards was full of coffee mugs. I immediately recognized one mug that was given to my grandmother when I was a child. It read, "Grandma You're Special." My uncle handed it to me and said, "Elise, take this home with you."

It was in fact the very mug my grandmother drank her tea out of every morning. For breakfast, Vavo would enjoy a slice of toast with butter and a cup of tea. For everyone else there were large, warm loaves of Portuguese Bread, a solid block of Portuguese butter, a big piece of Sao Jorge Portuguese cheese and hot tea from her glass Whistler tea pot. My sister and I both agree that my grandmother made the best tea.

So many hours were spent together in this little kitchen. For a moment I thought I heard the sound of her cooking and I waited to hear her say in Portuguese "Come, sit down and eat!"

Many of the stories I told my family over the years took place in that little kitchen, and now they could see it for themselves, exactly as it was then. My husband Mike was just as surprised as I was to see it so completely intact.

Within the basement there was a door that led to the laundry room and a large area where my grandmother would store pans, cookware and mason jars filled with freshly prepared canned goods, like crushed red peppers, beans and tomatoes. Hanging on a hook was my grandmother's apron and housecoat that my uncle said he "could never move or launder." Seeing, smelling and feeling the material was almost like touching my grandmother. I wept. I wanted to hang onto that moment forever. My uncle later sent this apron to me as a Christmas gift. It was one of the best, most thoughtful gifts I have ever received.

Near the washer and dryer was a wreath my mother had lovingly made for my grandmother when we moved to our townhouse in the mid 1980s. The wreath had four butterflies on it and each one was hand-painted and had our name on it.

Although it was difficult to go back to my grandmother's kitchen, we were all very happy that we had--especially me. May my grandmother's legacy of love and happiness continue. Mary Isabel Furtado will always be loved by family, friends and strangers alike.

Portuguese Kale Soup

Growing up in a Portuguese family, I very much enjoyed my grandmother's Portuguese Kale Soup, also known as "Caldo Verde." Portuguese Kale Soup is considered the national dish of Portugal by many, and for me, learning how to make it was like a rite of passage. My uncle George is always my go-to person when I'm trying to recreate my grandmother's recipes. It was he that I called when I was trying to put together the recipe for this special soup. My uncle was extremely close to my grandmother and I know that keeping my grandmother's legacy alive warms his heart.

This soup has always had a place at every holiday table.

1 large piece of beef roast (bone-in is best for flavor)

1 large bunch of kale, washed and chopped, with stalks removed but set aside for the stock.

1 pound of chourico links (Portuguese smoked sausage)

3 large white potatoes, peeled and cubed

2 large sweet potatoes, peeled and cubed

1 to 2 tablespoons Pimento Moida (fresh red crushed pepper) depending on your taste

2 teaspoon kosher salt, more or less your taste

1 teaspoon black pepper (to taste)

2 tablespoons garlic powder

2 tablespoons onion powder

1 cup elbow macaroni

Using a knife, make tiny slits in the chourico links.

Place the roast, chourico and kale stalks into a large soup pot. Add water three-quarters of the way up the pot. Bring the water to a boil, and then reduce heat a bit. Cook the stock for one hour.

Carefully remove the roast and the chourico and cut them into bite size pieces. Place the pieces back in the soup pan.

Add the white and sweet potatoes, chopped kale greens, salt and pepper, red crushed pepper and garlic and onion powders and cook for an additional hour.

At the last minute, add one cup of small macaroni and cook for five minutes.

Vavo's Pan Fried Fish and Red Gravy with Stewed Potatoes

"It's almost time to go home," I thought as I sat behind my school desk. As my mind wandered, I speculated what meal my grandmother would be preparing today. Perhaps she'd prepare one of my favorites like Spaghetti and Meatballs or Pan Fried Fish with Red Gravy, Stewed Potatoes and Boule!

How I loved my grandmother's meals! And her Boule was one of the most special of all of her treats. I would watch in awe as Vavo would make this flat bread on top of the stove. Once the soft white dough hit the heat, it bubbled up everywhere, and then turned brown and crispy before my eyes. I loved its crispy texture and its savory, almost smoky flavor. I could hardly wait to dunk it into the Red Gravy I loved so much!

I was so fortunate to live upstairs from my grandmother. I would faithfully knock on her door at the same time every day after school. Anxious to have a taste of what she'd been preparing, I'd rush downstairs as I was greeted by the incredible smells emanating from her kitchen. With great fervor, she would say in a Portuguese accent, "Come *linda* (which means pretty in Portuguese), sit down and eat."

For the next hour, she'd share with me the fruits of her labor. If I came early enough, I'd help her prepare some of the meal. There were times when I would just marvel at her amazing skills in the kitchen. Her heart poured out into every dish.

The time my grandmother invested in me helped to set the tenor for my adult life. My commitment to encouraging families to make memories by spending time together in the kitchen is a continuance of the legacy my grandmother left behind.

Under Vavo's tutelage, I learned not only the value of being an excellent cook, but that my grandmother and I had something very special in common; we loved people and we loved to feed them! The memories made in her kitchen have stayed with me throughout the years. There hasn't been one day that I don't think about her and all of the lessons she taught me. I never cook alone because her memory is always present.

Enjoying a meal that was once prepared by my grandmother is like stepping back in time. Many foods are referred to as "comfort foods" because they stimulate our five senses, bringing to mind the past and those who nurtured us with their loving care. Memories outlast a lifetime, so get into the kitchen and leave a legacy!

Vavo's Pan Fried Fish

2 pounds fresh cod, cut into serving pieces (remember that cod may shrink a bit in size when cooked)
Approximately ¾ cup unbleached all-purpose flour (just enough to coat both sides of the fish)
1 teaspoon kosher salt
½ teaspoon white pepper
¼ cup olive oil or enough to coat the bottom of your pan
2 yellow onions, peeled, halved and sliced
2 cloves of garlic, minced
½ cup ketchup
1 tablespoon salted butter
Salt and pepper to taste
Juice of one lemon
1/3 cup white distilled vinegar

Be sure to remove all of the bones from the fish. Combine the flour, salt and pepper on a plate with a fork. Coat your pieces of fish in the flour mixture and place them in a heated skillet coated with olive oil. Lightly brown each piece of cod on both sides, and then cook them until the fish feels firm when touched--about 8 minutes.

Once cooked, set the fish aside on a plate lined with paper towels. Add onions, garlic, ketchup, butter, lemon juice and vinegar to the pan. Watch your nose! The smell of the vinegar will grab you when it hits the pan! Cook the mixture for five minutes more, making sure to frequently stir to release the flavor in the bits at the bottom of the pan. If you want to thin the sauce out a bit, you can add a little water. I like my gravy on the thick side. Bring the gravy to a simmer and serve over your fish.

My Grandmother's Stewed Potatoes

My grandmother always served her pan-fried fish with stewed potatoes. The recipe calls for saffron, but if you find yourself without any on hand, you can use turmeric. Turmeric will not flavor your potatoes like saffron will, but it will give them a nice yellow color.

Like pasta, potatoes have a large amount of starch in them so be sure to use a large enough pan so that they have plenty of room to cook.

Feeds 4 hungry people

5 russet potatoes, peeled and cubed
1 bay leaf
2 cloves garlic
1 onion, sliced
1 teaspoon saffron threads
1 tablespoon fresh red crushed pepper or ½ teaspoon dried red pepper flakes
White pepper
Enough water to cover potatoes
Chopped fresh parsley for garnish

Bring all of the ingredients to a boil and cook them until the potatoes are fork-tender. Drain the potatoes, top with a fresh addition of parsley, and serve up right away. I remember my grandmother always using curly parsley. I typically use curly or Italian parsley. You can add a little more salt if needed. This is a wonderful accompaniment to Vavo's Portuguese fish! I can still see her making this in her kitchen!

Portuguese Stuffing

Portuguese stuffing has been a staple at each holiday meal or special family gathering since I was a child. Trust me, this is unlike any stuffing you've ever had before. I love to make it-- not only because it reminds me of my grandmother, mother and sister, but because my son Nathaniel now helps me every time I make it. Nathaniel helps me squeeze the water from the bread and stir the stuffing. We love to cook together while sharing the day's events! It is always a wonderful feeling when you can make people feel good with your culinary creations, but to include your family in the preparation is priceless.

As a contributor for the My Carolina Today show in North Carolina, I was thrilled when I got to share my grandmother's stuffing recipe with viewers. No one had ever seen or tried this type of stuffing before and I knew they would adore it. We loved watching the prerecorded segments in the comfort of our home. The day the stuffing segment aired, I knew how excited my grandmother would have been to have seen it. I imagined her in heaven calling her family members and friends over and saying--in her Portuguese accent of course--"C'mon, c'mon, hurry up, that'sa my granddaughter . . . my granddaughter Elise is making my stuffing on television! And look there's a picture of me on the counter!" It makes me smile and tear up just thinking about it!

My grandmother always used 73% ground beef, but that is difficult to come by these days, so I typically use 80% and it works out just fine. I hope you enjoy this recipe with your family during the holidays.

5 day-old Portuguese or Italian breads
3 pounds 80% ground beef
1 bunch scallions, chopped
1 green bell pepper, chopped
1/2 cup fresh parsley, chopped
1 cup vegetable oil
2 tablespoons each kosher salt, ground black pepper, garlic powder, onion powder and fresh red crushed pepper (if using dry only use ½ to ¾ teaspoon)
4 large eggs
½ cup fresh lemon juice
1/3 or more cup paprika

Soak one or two pieces of bread at a time in water, and then squeeze the liquid out very well. Otherwise, your bread will be soggy by the time you squeeze the water out.

In a large Dutch oven, cook the ground beef, scallions, bell pepper, and parsley in vegetable oil for 30 minutes, stirring often. Remove the Dutch oven from the heat. Add in your wet bread and mix it well with or a heavy wooden spoon or your hands. Be careful if using your hands, it's hot in places. I sometimes let it cool a bit before adding the bread.

Add in the eggs and lemon juice. Mix everything very well. Place the stuffing back over the heat and cook it, stirring often, until it's sticky--about 15 minutes. Add in the paprika until the color of the stuffing changes to a light orange. Season the stuffing well with salt and white pepper, spread it a baking pan and bake it in a 350 degree F oven for 30 minutes.

We typically make this recipe days in advance. To store your stuffing, once it has been placed in the baking pan, cover it with heavy duty aluminum foil and freeze. When you're ready to serve your stuffing, thaw it out in the refrigerator, then place in the oven.

A note: This stuffing is also used to make Stuffed Quahogs, the quintessential appetizer served throughout Southeastern Massachusetts. In place of ground beef, chopped quahogs are used.

Vavo's Spaghetti and Meatballs

Another benefit of living in the apartment above Vavo's house was that the smells from her kitchen would travel up into our home, and we always knew what she was making. Between my grandmother's and parents' cooking I was forever surrounded by the scent of good food and the feeling of being loved and cared for!

On certain evenings, around dinner time, our telephone would ring in our apartment. My mother would answer it and tell me that my grandmother was calling for me. Vavo was serving one of my favorite meals, spaghetti and meatballs! With a huge smile, I'd give my mother a look that said 'Mom, I'll be back!'

You can imagine how many calories I consumed having a grandmother who cooked so well and a mother committed to sit-down family dinners. I was allowed to eat two dinners throughout my childhood if I wanted to but I had to ride my bike for one hour each day. It was worth it!

My grandmother's spaghetti and meatballs had such a unique flavor; the sauce, or gravy, was the perfect balance of sweet and spicy. I scarfed it up and felt full both in belly and soul.

One of the canned goods found in my grandmothers' basement kitchen was "Pimento Moida" or crushed red pepper. The crushed red pepper was what gave this dish its unique spicy flavor. Each year my parents would help my grandmother crush and can the peppers. On that day children were not allowed in the house. A sign that read "Do Not Enter-Canning Peppers" would be taped onto my grandmother's front door. On those days, I knew to obey and not to enter. Crushing and canning the peppers would take hours of effort before the task was done.

The heat from the peppers was so intense that anyone who helped with the canning had to wear gloves and mask their faces. If you weren't careful you could badly burn your eyes, skin and throat. When the canning was completed, Vavo's shelves would be jam-packed with canning jars filled with Pimento Moida. Today I have my fresh red crushed pepper shipped to me from my hometown of Fall River, Massachusetts.

I have substituted dried red pepper flakes for fresh Pimento Moida only when in a pinch. When doing so, I use a fraction of what I would use with the wet mixture. You may go to my website (cookingwithelise.com) to find a store in my hometown that will ship this amazing ingredient right to your door!

Meatballs

1 pound ground beef
2 large eggs
2 tablespoons ketchup or chili sauce
1 tablespoon yellow mustard
½ cup grated Parmesan cheese
1 tablespoon Worcestershire Sauce
2 teaspoons garlic powder
2 teaspoons onion powder
1 teaspoon kosher salt
½ teaspoon white pepper
Handful of fresh chopped parsley
About 1 cup of fresh white bread soaked in a little milk
A little dried breadcrumbs if needed

Combine all of the ingredients and form them into uniformly-sized meatballs and bake in a 350 degree F oven until they are a little browned. My Vavo always fried her meatballs in a pan, but I like to bake mine.

Do not cook the meatballs all the way through. You just want them to brown on the outside so that when you place them in the sauce, they will not fall apart. As they continue cooking in the sauce, the meatballs will add an immense amount of flavor to it.

While the meatballs are browning, begin making Vavo's spaghetti sauce:

My Grandmother's Spaghetti Sauce

3 tablespoons Portuguese, extra-virgin or Spanish olive oil
½ green bell pepper, chopped
1 large yellow onion, chopped
4 cloves of garlic, minced
1 (28-oz can) crushed tomatoes
1 (14-oz can) stewed tomatoes, broken up with your fingers
1 (6-oz can) tomato paste
2 bay leaves, dried or fresh
Garlic and onion powder (my grandmother would add it on top to look like she'd dusted the sauce with it)
2 teaspoons kosher salt
1 tablespoon Italian seasonings
½ teaspoon dried red crushed pepper or 1 tablespoon fresh Pimento Moida
A pinch of sugar to round out the flavors (sugar will help cut the acidity from the tomatoes)
1 pound spaghetti
Salt to taste

In a large skillet or Dutch oven, sauté the onions and green peppers in olive oil until they're softened. Add in your garlic and cook the mixture for a minute more. Add in the next ten ingredients. Finally, add in your meatballs. Simmer the sauce and meatballs together for one hour. Stir the sauce from time to time to keep it from burning on the bottom of the pan.

Cook your pasta in a large pot of salted water until it's soft and pliable, yet slightly firm. Enjoy!

Malasadas (Portuguese Fried Doughnuts)

Ah, the smell of Malasadas! I can still see my grandmother devotedly preparing these fried doughnuts. Malasadas, or Portuguese fried dough treats, are made for very special occasions like Easter and Christmas. My mother told me that on the mornings of her childrens' weddings, my grandmother would prepare a special breakfast feast for everyone, which always included dozens of hot Malasadas.

The marriage of shortening and fried dough created the most incredible sound. Once the doughnuts were golden brown they were immediately placed in a large brown paper bag filled with granulated sugar. As a child I often got to shake up the doughnuts in the bag. When you heard that sound you knew it was time to open wide!

It amazes me that my grandmother was able to add the making of this treat to the already busy schedule of a wedding day. Like me, cooking was never a chore for my grandmother. My grandmother adored feeding others, and was never overwhelmed by the amount of work or time it took to prepare food.

Watching my grandmother work in the kitchen was like observing an artist-- only she used food and kitchen tools in place of brushes and canvases. I simply loved watching my Vavo cook, and for me, it was magical. Vavo was an expert in the kitchen. Although we rarely spoke, she taught me countless lessons in the heart of her home.

My grandmother also reserved a very special day for making Malasadas. Tony, my grandmother's son, passed away when he was only four years old. Tony loved his Mama's Malasadas, so my grandmother would make them every year in honor of her precious boy's birthday.

Many Catholic churches in Fall River host celebrations called "feasts" like the Holy Ghost and the harvest festivals. Many of the older Portuguese women who are experts at making Malasadas donate their time to make thousands of them in one weekend for the parishioners to savor and enjoy. Follow the smell of fried dough and you'll find lengthy lines of individuals waiting to get their hands on these warm doughnuts.

Growing up in Fall River, I enjoyed going to these feasts. There were always carousel rides, games, raffles, auctions, and best of all—delicious Portuguese food and drinks!

1 ¼ cup warm milk
1 tablespoon granulated sugar
2 ½ teaspoon kosher salt
1 stick salted butter
1 tablespoon dry active yeast
6 large eggs, slightly beaten
6 cups unbleached all-purpose flour
1 tablespoon softened butter
3 cups Crisco, or canola oil (I recommend Crisco)
2 cups or more granulated sugar (place in large brown paper bag)

Begin by scalding 1 cup of the milk in a medium-sized saucepan over medium-high heat. Stir in the sugar, salt and butter and immediately remove them from the heat.

In a small saucepan, warm the remaining 1/4 cup of milk over medium heat. Remove the pan from the heat and mix in the yeast. Let the mixture stand for 5 minutes, then stir until the yeast dissolves into the milk.

In a large mixing bowl, combine the two milk mixtures with the beaten eggs.

Gradually add in the flour, beating it with a wooden spoon until it becomes stiff. Move the dough to a floured board and knead it until it's smooth and elastic. Form the dough into a ball and place it in bowl coated with ¼ cup of olive oil. Turn the dough so that it is lightly coated with the olive oil. Cover the bowl with a towel and let it rise in a warm place until it has doubled in size, approximately 2 hours.

Meanwhile, in a deep pot, heat the remaining 3 cups of corn oil or shortening to 350 degrees F. Break off golf ball sized pieces of the dough and stretch them into an oval or round shape. Fry them in batches in the hot oil until they're golden brown, turning them over once as they cook. Using tongs, carefully remove Malasadas from oil, immediately place in paper bag, shake up to fully coat with sugar!

Massa Sovada (Portuguese Sweet Bread)

Makes 2 large round loaves or several small rolls.

My grandmother made the best Portuguese sweet bread--known as "massa"--several times a year. Because eggs represent life, large brown hardboiled eggs were baked into the bread only at Easter time. Massa with eggs baked in it is referred to as Folar da Páscoa. My Vavo made dozens of this bread in different sizes, including little individual breads with one egg in them.

I suspect that my Vavo learned how to make massa in the small village of Livremente and later with her stepmother in the States. My grandmother never had recipes, nor did she ever write anything down. She simply created remarkable food, which is a tell-tale sign of a gifted cook. The secret to being an extraordinary cook is undeniably **love** -- pure and simple.

Vavo would spend hours downstairs in her kitchen with her apron on, mixing, kneading and forming her breads by hand. She would make several large round loaves of bread, as well as braided breads and little breads. Various large bowls covered in dishtowels could be found strategically placed in warm, draft-free areas all over her immaculate, well-used kitchen.

Although my grandmother's recipe was never written down, I have done my best to replicate it over the years. One day during Easter, after years of trying to get the massa just right, my children and I finally had a breakthrough. Our massa tasted just like hers, and the texture was just right! Although this recipe takes some time to prepare, let rise and bake, it is definitely worth it.

10 cups (more or less) unbleached all-purpose flour
3 tablespoons active dry yeast, plus one teaspoon granulated sugar
½ cup warm water (105 to 115 degrees F)
9 large eggs (white or brown), at room temperature
1 cup salted butter
2 teaspoons canola oil
1 cup whole milk
2¼ granulated sugar
Zest of two large lemons
Egg wash (one egg mixed with a splash milk)

Take your eggs out of the refrigerator at least two hours before using. In a bowl, dissolve your yeast in ½ cup of warm water with one teaspoon of granulated sugar. Allow your yeast to "proof"—that is, turn bubbly and creamy. Note the amazing smell!

Beat nine eggs until they are light, fluffy and a beautiful creamy yellow. Add your "sponge"—a term for proofed yeast--to the eggs and mix in just enough flour to make a batter. Cover the batter with a dishcloth and/or blanket until it forms bubbles. In the meantime, melt the butter over low heat. Add the canola oil to the butter and mix it in. Add in the milk, a pinch of salt and the lemon zest.

When the bread batter has formed bubbles, add the granulated sugar into the butter mixture. Mix well. Add in the remaining flour one cup at a time, mixing well each time. If your dough is very sticky, don't panic! It's supposed to be! When it becomes too difficult to stir the dough with a wooden spoon, it's ready. Pour it out onto a floured surface (I use my island). Knead, adding the remaining flour little by little until the dough is smooth and not too sticky. Resist adding too much flour. You want a light and fluffy bread in the end.

Cover your bread dough with a towel. Let it rise until it doubles in size.

Shape the loaves of bread into the sizes you want and place them in buttered loaf pans.

Cover the dough with a towel until it has doubled in size. Allow the dough to rise a second time. When ready to bake brush each loaf with the egg wash to achieve a bright and shiny crust.

Bake for one hour on the low oven rack at 275 degrees F.

Note: Let the dough rise (ball form and bread pan form) for about 4 to 6 hours.

The Significance of Folar da Pascoa (Easter Bread)

One Easter weekend, while kneading sweet bread dough with my children, I suddenly remembered exactly what my grandmother's hands looked and felt like as she would lovingly knead the dough in her huge Massa pan. Memories of the care she took making the bread came flooding back to me.

As I kneaded, I could see my Vavo placing the dough into the large pan and working it for what seemed like forever. She always made several breads at once, which took a great deal of muscle! I was only making two sweet breads and my arms were already beginning to tire.

I recalled my grandmother cutting a sign of the cross in the top of the dough, covering the pan with a large clean dishtowel, laying her rosary beads over top and then setting the pan in a draft-free place to rise for a second time. Like my grandmother, I too cut a cross in the top of my dough and carefully set it aside to rise.

When I checked on the dough hours later, I noticed that once it rose, the cross had disappeared. While my boys looked on, I began to weep. I suddenly realized what the bread signified--the death and resurrection of my Lord and Savior, Jesus Christ.

The large pan was like the tomb Jesus' body was laid in. The dish towel that covered and protected the dough was like the shroud Jesus was wrapped in after His death.

The disappearance of the cross showed the victory of life over death that we can all share through the resurrection of Jesus.

My grandmother and I shared a bond that went beyond words. What Vavo did in the kitchen and what I now do echo eternal truths.

The recipe for Easter Bread is the same as the Massa Sovada with the addition of five whole brown eggs that are cooked into the bread. If you are baking massa with eggs (Folar da Pascoa) for the Easter season, after the first rise and before the second rise place the dough into the shapes or pans that you prefer, and then carefully push your whole raw eggs into the top of the dough. The dough will rise around the eggs.

Notes and Memories

INDIA

Naan Bread

Chicken Tikka Masala

Infused Basmati Rice

Raita, a Cucumber Yogurt Sauce

The aroma that radiates from your kitchen as you make Indian flatbread is enough to send you over the edge. Our family resists digging right into this bread as soon as it is taken out of the oven because a brushing of melted butter, garlic and parsley is well worth the wait!

This Naan Bread was part of my winning signature dish for the 2010 Meals on Wheels Chef's Challenge. In addition to the delicious Naan Bread, I presented the judges with my Chicken Tikka Masala, Infused Basmati Rice, and Raita, a refreshing cucumber yogurt sauce.

I was up against stiff competition--trained chefs who really presented me with a challenge. But in the end the judges declared that it was the "love" found in my food that made me victorious. Don't ever doubt yourself!

Naan Bread

I don't know many folks who have a traditional Indian clay oven, but the use of a baking stone in your regular oven works wonderfully!

Serves 6

2 teaspoons dry active yeast
¾ cup lukewarm water
2 cups unbleached bread flour, plus extra for rolling out your dough
1 teaspoon salt
1 teaspoon granulated sugar
1/8 teaspoon baking soda
2 tablespoons canola oil
2½ tablespoons plain yogurt
2 tablespoons melted butter

Dissolve the active dry yeast in lukewarm water and let it sit for a few minutes until the mixture becomes frothy. Your yeast is now ready to go to work for you!

In a bowl combine flour, sugar, salt and baking soda and mix them well. Now add the oil and yogurt.

Add in the yeast mixture and stir with your hands making a soft dough.

Knead the dough until it's smooth. Place the dough in a greased bowl and cover it with a dish towel. Keep the dough in a warm, draft-free place for about three hours or until it doubles in size.

Thirty minutes before you are ready to bake your Naan, place your baking stone in the oven and preheat your oven to 500 degrees F.

Knead your dough for about two to three minutes, and then divide it into six equal parts.

Take each piece of dough and roll it into an 8-inch oval shape. Dust each oval lightly with dry flour to help with the rolling.

Before putting the Naan in your oven, lightly wet your hands, pick up the rolled Naan, and flip them between your palms and place onto your baking/pizza stone into the oven.

You should be able to fit about 3 Naan breads on one baking stone at a time. The Naan will bake quickly and only take about 2 to 3 minutes, depending upon your oven. Keep an eye on these breads because they burn quickly under the high temperature.

Once your Naan are golden brown, remove them from the oven and brush them lightly with butter.

It's best to put your stone back in the oven for a couple of minutes before baking the next batch of Naan bread. This keeps the stone hot, which simulates a traditional Indian clay oven.

Chicken Tikka Masala

Yogurt Marinade

1 cup plain yogurt
1 tablespoon lemon juice
2 teaspoons ground cumin
1 teaspoon ground cinnamon
2 teaspoons cayenne pepper
2 teaspoons freshly ground black pepper
1 tablespoon minced fresh ginger
1 teaspoon kosher salt
4 to 5 boneless skinless chicken breast, cut into 1-inch pieces

Curry Sauce

1 tablespoon butter
1 clove garlic, minced
2 teaspoons ground cumin
½ teaspoon cayenne pepper
1 teaspoon ground ginger
2 teaspoons paprika
1 teaspoon ground cloves
2 teaspoons garam masala, found in most grocery stores.
Salt to taste
1 (8-ounce) can tomato sauce
1 cup evaporated skim milk
¼ cup chopped fresh cilantro

In a large bowl, combine the yogurt, lemon juice, cumin, cinnamon, cayenne pepper, black pepper, ginger and salt. Stir in your chicken, cover it, and refrigerate it for at least 1 hour. It's really best if you marinate it overnight.

When you're ready to bake, remove the chicken from the marinade and place onto a broiler pan. Broil for about 5 minutes--just to dry out the yogurt a bit.

Begin making your curry sauce, by melting your butter in a sauté pan. Add in the garlic. Stir it for one minute. Add cumin, cayenne pepper, ginger, paprika, cloves, garam masala, and salt and cook for another minute, stirring frequently. Be careful not to let the garlic and spices burn. Add in the tomato sauce, evaporated milk, and cilantro. Finish cooking your chicken in your colorful, fragrant curry sauce for about 15 to 20 minutes. This is a great meal to make ahead of time!

Infused Basmati Rice

2 cups Basmati rice
1 ½ cups water
2 tablespoons butter
2 cinnamon sticks
2 bay leaves
Juice of one lime
1 teaspoon kosher salt
Handful of golden raisins, optional
Toasted cashews, optional garnish

Combine all ingredients and follow your rice cooker instructions.

If you don't have a rice cooker, bring the water, butter, cinnamon, bay leaves, lime juice and salt to a boil. Add in the rice, lower the heat, and cover. Simmer the rice for about 20 minutes, or until the rice has absorbed the water completely.

Topping this rice with toasted cashews adds color, rich flavor and a crunchy texture. I toast my nuts in a dry pan, for just a few minutes, watching and stirring constantly. Nuts contain natural oils and can burn easily if you're not careful, so please be attentive, stirring the whole time.

Raita, a Cool Cucumber Yogurt Sauce

Raita makes a cool contrast to spicy dishes like Chicken Tikka Masala.

2 cups non-fat Greek yogurt
1 medium cucumber, grated with liquid squeezed out
2 green onions, chopped
1 tablespoon cilantro, chopped
½ cup fresh mint leaves, chopped
¼ teaspoon ground cumin
Dash of pepper
1 clove garlic, minced
1 inch of ginger root, grated
Zest and juice of one lemon
½ teaspoon kosher salt or to taste
¼ teaspoon freshly ground black pepper

There could not be a simpler recipe; just combine all of the ingredients and refrigerate them.

ENGLAND

Rustic Brown Bread

Cottage Pie with Onion Gravy

Mushy Peas

English Bread Pudding with Caramel Sauce

While studying for his bachelor's degree in electrical engineering at Worcester Polytechnic Institute in Worcester, Massachusetts, my very handsome (if I do say so myself) soon-to-be husband was offered the opportunity to study abroad. Michael spent three months working on an engineering project in London, England. He would sometimes call me from a red telephone box (or booth) in the center of town.

Knowing how very much our family loves history, Michael dreamt of taking us to England one day. In 2006, we finally had the pleasure of going. While in England we enjoyed the hustle and bustle of London, the picturesque views of the countryside with its thatched roofs and green fields, and the country's remarkable history. We did a great deal of walking! Walking was a good thing because we also enjoyed a good number of chocolate-filled croissants! Did I just admit that?

One of my favorite moments in England occurred during our very first day there. We were headed to Picadilly Circus for fish and chips when Mike took an alternate route. He wanted to surprise me. As we turned a corner he said, "I want to show you something." He had taken me to the spot where he used to call me from the red box! Sadly, the red box had been replaced with an immense building. But I do believe that was one of the most thoughtful gestures anyone has ever made for me!

While in England we enjoyed many dishes, including mushy peas--a traditional English side dish-- and shepherd's pie. For over two hundred years, shepherd's pie has been served on many a table in Ireland and England. Warm, savory and hearty, shepherd's pie was the perfect meal after a long day of sightseeing!

Shepherd's pie is inexpensive, easy to make and delicious. Although this pie is traditionally made with lamb, here in the United States, ground beef is most commonly used. In England, folks would consider a pie made with ground beef a cottage pie.

I sometimes make this pie with ground turkey, and it is just delicious! I also find that onion gravy makes a great addition to the pie—regardless of meat choice--but it is optional. While this pie is typically made in a 9 x 13-inch baking pan or dish, you can make it in individual ramekins for special occasions. My garlic mashed potatoes make the most wonderful topping. Adding brown bread and crumb cakes—two other very common and delicious English dishes—to this meal really makes it complete!

Rustic Brown Bread

Makes 1 loaf

1 tablespoon dry active yeast
2 cups unbleached bread flour
1¼ cups whole wheat flour
1 tablespoon kosher salt
1 cup plus 3 tablespoons warm water
2 tablespoons softened, salted butter or olive oil

Mix the flour, salt and yeast together in your large bowl or mixer. Add in the warm water. Using a wooden spoon or your mixer's paddle attachment, stir the ingredients until they're just combined. Turn the dough onto a floured counter and knead it until it's smooth and springy. This may take approximately 10 minutes. Add in a little extra all-purpose flour if necessary.

Lightly oil a large, clean bowl and let the dough rise in a warm place until it doubles in size which takes about 40 minutes. Punch the dough down and shape the loaf. Let the loaf rest until it doubles in size again--about 30 minutes. Preheat the oven to 425 degrees F. Bake the bread for 35 minutes, or until the bottom of the loaf sounds hollow when tapped. Cool the bread before slicing.

Cottage Pie with Onion Gravy

Begin by making the mashed potato topping.

My Garlic Mashed Potatoes

3 heads garlic in skin, tops cut off
3 tablespoon olive oil
2 pounds potatoes, peeled and cubed
1 stick butter, cubed
½ to ¾ cup 2% milk
Salt and white pepper, to taste

Preheat the oven to 450 degrees F.

Place the head of garlic inside a foil pouch and drizzle it with olive oil. Seal the garlic and place it in the oven to roast for 35 to 40 minutes, or until tender and golden brown. Remove the garlic from the oven and allow it to cool. Squeeze from the head and place in a small bowl. Using a fork, mash the garlic until smooth.

Be sure to cut your potatoes in uniformed sizes so that they cook correctly. Place the potatoes in a pot of salted water and bring them to a boil. Reduce the heat to a simmer and cook the potatoes until they're fork tender--about 12 to 15 minutes.

Remove the pan from the heat and drain the potatoes. Place the potatoes back in the pot and return them to the heat for a minute to dry the potatoes. Remove the potatoes from the heat and add in the garlic and butter. Using a hand-held masher, mash the butter and garlic into the potatoes. Add in the milk a little at a time and stir until you get your desired texture. The potatoes should still be sort of lumpy. Season them with salt and pepper, and then set them aside while you make your meat filling.

Turkey and Vegetable Filling

1 yellow onion, diced
2 carrots, diced
2 celery stalks, diced
3 cloves garlic, minced
½ teaspoon chopped rosemary
1 ½ pounds ground turkey (I use 7% fat) or beef
1 teaspoon kosher salt
¼ teaspoon ground black pepper
2 tablespoons unbleached all-purpose flour (can be omitted)
2 tablespoons Worcestershire sauce
½ cup low sodium beef broth

In a skillet, sauté your onions, carrots, celery, garlic and rosemary until tender. Add in your ground turkey and cook it until it's browned through. Add salt, pepper and flour. Allow the flour to cook for a minute. Now add the Worcestershire sauce and beef broth. Let the mixture thicken for a minute or so.

Place the meat mixture in your baking dish and, spread the mashed potatoes on top. You can use your fork to make pretty designs, which will brown up nicely in the oven. **This is a great time to get the kids in the kitchen to help!**

Bake your pie in a preheated 375 degree F oven for about 30 to 40 minutes, or until the potatoes have browned a bit on top. I broil my Cottage Pie at the last minute (just for a couple of minutes or so) to get a lovely dark brown color on top. I watch it very carefully!

While your pie is baking, you can make this easy Onion Gravy to serve over the top. Or, you can just eat it as is-either way is delicious! Happy eating!

Onion Gravy

1 medium sized onion, thinly sliced
3 tablespoons canola oil
3 tablespoons unbleached all-purpose flour
1 cup good red wine
2 cups beef broth
Kosher salt and freshly ground black pepper

In a medium saucepan over medium heat, sauté the onions in oil until they're translucent--about 5 minutes. Add in the flour and stir to evenly coat it with oil. Slowly whisk in the wine and then the broth.

Simmer the gravy until it thickens and season it with salt and pepper to taste. Enjoy this gravy with your Cottage Pie—or with any of your favorite meats!

Mushy Peas

Please do not be turned off by the name. These peas are served all over England, and are one of my personal favorite side dishes. This version is quicker than most recipes because we are using frozen peas to save time and money. You can also cook dried peas that have been soaked overnight, but frozen peas work very well.

1 (10-ounce) package frozen green peas
¼ cup half-and-half
1 tablespoon salted butter
1 teaspoon kosher salt
½ teaspoon freshly ground black pepper

Add your frozen peas to pot of lightly salted water and bring them to a boil. Cook them for 3 minutes, or until they're tender.

Drain the peas and place them in a blender or large food processor. Add in the half-and-half, butter, salt and pepper and process them until they're well-blended but not completely smooth.

This will be a thick mixture, but I do like the texture of smooth peas with a few peas left whole. Adjust your seasonings to taste, and serve the peas immediately.

If you don't own a food processor, get the kids in the kitchen and put your masher to good use!

English Bread Pudding with Caramel Sauce

In this recipe, cubes of dry bread are soaked in thick and creamy custard and adorned with a homemade caramel sauce--making what I hope will be one of the best bread puddings you will ever enjoy.

Bread Pudding

8 cups cubed day-old bread (dry bread soaks up the moisture better)
9 large eggs
2¼ cups milk
1¾ cups heavy cream
1 cup granulated sugar
¾ cup butter, melted
1 tablespoon pure vanilla extract
Zest of one large orange
Zest of one large lemon
2 teaspoons ground cinnamon
½ teaspoon freshly ground nutmeg

Caramel Sauce

1 cup granulated sugar
¼ cup water
1 tablespoon orange juice
2 tablespoon salted butter
1 cup heavy cream

Place the bread cubes in a greased 9 x 13-inch baking dish. In a large bowl, whisk the eggs, milk, cream, sugar, melted butter, vanilla extract, orange and lemon zests, cinnamon and nutmeg together.

Pour the custard mixture evenly over your bread cubes. Press the bread cubes down a bit to ensure all of the cubes soak up the egg mixture.

Bake the bread cubes, uncovered, at 350 degrees F for 40 to 45 minutes, or until a knife inserted in the center comes out clean. Let the pudding stand before cutting into.

Meanwhile, in a small saucepan, bring the sugar, water and orange juice to a boil until it turns a lovely amber color. Stir in remaining butter until melted. Add in the cream. Remove the sauce from the heat, and serve it with the bread pudding.

Notes and Memories

IRELAND

Irish Soda Bread

Irish Beef Stew

Colcannon

Traditional Irish Scones

Blueberry Peach Crumb Cake

My husband is one quarter Irish, so our family loves celebrating St. Patrick's Day. We always invite others to join us for some of our family's favorite Irish recipes. However these recipes are too good to enjoy only once a year so we eat some of them quite often!

Irish Soda Bread

4 cups unbleached all-purpose flour, plus extra for currants
4 tablespoons sugar
1 teaspoon baking soda
1 ½ teaspoons kosher salt
4 tablespoons (1/2 stick) cold unsalted butter, cut into 1/2-inch dice
1 ¾ cups cold buttermilk, shaken
1 large egg, lightly beaten
Zest of one orange or lemon
1 cup dried currants or raisins

Preheat the oven to 375 degrees F. Line a baking stone or sheet pan with parchment paper.

Combine the flour, sugar, baking soda, and salt in the bowl of an electric mixer fitted with the paddle attachment. Add the butter and mix on low speed until the butter is mixed into the flour. Or, if you don't have a mixer, or don't feel quite up to lugging yours out, you can use a regular bowl and a wooden spoon.

With a fork, lightly beat the buttermilk, egg and orange zest together in a measuring cup. With the mixer on low speed, slowly add the buttermilk mixture to the flour mixture. In a small bowl coat the currants with 1 tablespoon of flour to prevent them from sinking in the bread. Mix into the dough. The dough will be very wet.

Dump the dough onto a well-floured board and knead it a few times into a round loaf. Place the loaf on the prepared baking stone or sheet pan and lightly cut an X into the top of the bread with a serrated knife. Bake the bread for 45 to 55 minutes, or until a cake tester comes out clean. When you tap the bottom of the loaf, it should have a hollow sound. In the world of crusty bread, hollow means done!

Cool the bread on a baking rack. Serve it warm or at room temperature—it tastes great both ways.

Irish Beef Stew

3 pounds beef or lamb stew meat cut into bite size pieces
1 tablespoon canola oil
6 stalks celery, cut into ½-inch slices
2 large yellow onions, cut into ½-inch cubes
4 cloves garlic, minced
2 teaspoons dried rosemary
2 teaspoons dried thyme
1 bunch fresh parsley
48 ounces beef stock, reserve ½ cup for slurry* later on
12 ounces Guinness stout
1 cup of good red wine
2 tablespoons Worcestershire sauce
3 large Russet potatoes, peeled and cubed
3 large carrots, peeled and sliced
2 teaspoons cornstarch
Salt and freshly ground black pepper, to taste
Freshly chopped parsley, optional garnish

Season the meat with salt and pepper, and then brown it in a little oil. Add in the onions, garlic and celery to the pan and sauté, stirring often. Add in the Guinness, red wine and Worcestershire sauce and bring them to a boil. Stir, making sure that you scrape up (or deglaze) any bits at the bottom of the pan – this is where all of the flavor is. Reduce the heat to very low. Simmer the meat for 1½ hours or until it's tender, stirring occasionally. Add in the potatoes and carrots, then cook the stew for another 20 to 30 minutes or until the vegetables are tender.

When everything is cooked the way you'd like, make a slurry by combining cornstarch with the reserved beef broth in a small bowl. Stir the slurry into the stew while the heat is on and continue to stir until the stew thickens slightly. Taste the stew to check your seasonings. Add salt and pepper if needed, then remove the stew from the heat and stir in parsley.

A "slurry" is a thin paste of water and starch (flour, cornstarch or arrowroot), which is added to hot soups, stews and sauces as a thickener. After the slurry has been added, the mixture is typically stirred and cooked for a few minutes in order to thicken and lose any raw taste.

Colcannon

2 pounds russet potatoes
1 stick salted butter
1 ¼ cups warm half-and-half
Freshly ground black pepper
½ pound bacon, diced
1 head cabbage, cored and finely shredded (you can also use curly kale)
1 large shallot, minced
4 scallions, finely chopped
Chopped parsley leaves, for garnish
Touch of good malt vinegar

Boil the potatoes whole with their skins on in salted water until they're tender. Allow the potatoes to cool just enough so that you can then peel them. Add in the butter, warm half-and-half and spices and mash the potatoes with a masher.

This recipe calls for thickly mashed potatoes. Boiling potatoes whole and with the skin on results in a less watery mash. In addition, I find half-and-half to be the perfect choice for this recipe, as milk can make it a little too watery and the flavor of cream will dominate the dish.

Cook your bacon in a large saucepan and remove it when it's nice and crisp. Leave a good amount of the rendered bacon fat in the pan, and then add in the scallions, cabbage and shallots. Cook the cabbage or kale until it's tender.

Add the mashed potatoes and reserved cooked bacon to the cabbage or kale. Mix it well and season it properly with salt, black pepper and a hint of malt vinegar. Sprinkle the dish with additional chopped parsley for a pretty green garnish.

Traditional Irish Scones

These scones aren't just for St. Patrick's Day! I bake them for guests at tea parties, for brunches, for friends and family during extended visits or when we're simply in the mood for a nice cup of tea and a scone.

Makes 8 large or 16 smaller scones

2 cups unbleached all-purpose flour
3 tablespoons brown sugar
2 teaspoon aluminum-free baking powder

½ teaspoon baking soda
½ teaspoon kosher salt
¼ cup cold butter, cut into pieces
1 cup raisins or currants
1 egg yolk
1 cup heavy whipping cream
Raw sugar for top of scones

In a food processor, combine the flour, brown sugar, baking powder, baking soda and salt. Pulse the mixture a couple of times. Add in pieces of cold butter and pulse until it resembles coarse crumbs. Pour the mixture into a large bowl. Toss in the plump, beautiful raisins and the aromatic orange or lemon zest. Move the raisins around in the dry mixture a little.

In a small bowl, combine the egg yolk and whipping cream. Add them to the dry mixture and stir it with a fork just until everything is combined. Be sure to not over mix. The mixture will appear dry, but is not. Turn the mixture onto a lightly floured board or counter. This is where the fun begins! Gently press the mixture together until it can be easily kneaded. Don't you just love the feeling of dough? Knead the dough for 2 minutes by folding and gently pressing the dough together until it is nearly smooth. Roll out into an 8-inch circle. Cut into 8 large beautiful wedges.

Place the scones on a greased baking stone or cookie sheet. Sprinkle raw sugar over the top of the scones. Bake the scones in a preheated 400 degree F oven for 10 to 12 minutes or until they're lightly browned on top. Then, enjoy!

Blueberry Peach Crumb Cake

Blueberries and peaches make the perfect combination in this traditional buttermilk crumb cake. Delicious by itself, this cake is even better with a dollop of vanilla or cinnamon ice cream; I promise you will love it as much as I do!

Crumb Cake

¼ cup softened butter
¾ cup light brown sugar
1 egg
2 cup unbleached all-purpose flour
1 tablespoon baking powder
½ teaspoon kosher salt
1 cup buttermilk
1 teaspoon pure vanilla extract
2 cup fresh blueberries
2 peaches, peeled and sliced (optional)

In a mixer or regular bowl, mix together the butter, brown sugar and egg until they're smooth. In a separate bowl, combine your dry ingredients. Add these into the wet mixture and stir them just until everything is lightly combined. Add the buttermilk and vanilla extract. Stir them in until they're well incorporated. Carefully fold in your plump, sweet blueberries. Carefully spread mixture in a greased 9 x 13-inch baking pan. Insert peach slices every couple of inches into your batter.

Make your topping and sprinkle it on top.

Topping

¼ cup cold salted butter
½ cup light brown sugar
1/3 cup unbleached all-purpose flour
½ teaspoon ground cinnamon

Bake in a 350 degree F oven for 35 minutes, or until a toothpick inserted in the center comes out clean.

Spain

Tortilla de Esparragos, Papas, y Cebollas (Asparagus, Potato and Onion Omelet)

Ensalada (Spanish Salad)

Paella

Spanish Flan (Custard)

A tapas party—a party where a number of different appetizers are served, rather than a full meal--is an easy, fun and inexpensive way to spend time with friends. Light some candles, play some beautiful Spanish guitar music and have plenty of small plates for tasting.

Tortilla de Esparragos, Papas, y Cebollas   (Asparagus, Potato and Onion Omelet)

¼ cup Spanish olive oil, plus 1 tablespoon
1 pound fresh asparagus, steamed and cut into 2-inch pieces
2 medium-sized white potatoes, peeled and sliced in half moon shapes, about 1/8-inches thick
6 large eggs
1 large yellow onion, cut in half and thinly sliced
3 cloves garlic, mashed
¼ cup freshly chopped cilantro, optional
Kosher salt and pepper to taste

Heat the olive oil in a 9 or 10-inch non-stick omelet pan. Heat the mashed garlic in the pan just until it's golden and then discard it. It only serves to infuse the oil with garlic flavor. Add the potato slices to the oil and cook them over medium heat.

After about five minutes, add in the onions. Lift and turn the potatoes and onions until they are cooked. Once the potatoes are tender, add the asparagus and mix thoroughly.

In a large bowl, beat together the eggs, salt and pepper. Using a slotted spoon, scoop the potatoes, asparagus and onions into the eggs. Add a tablespoon of olive oil to the skillet and add in the egg mixture, spreading it evenly. Cook it over medium heat. Shake the pan as the eggs cook.

Once the eggs spring from the side of the pan, invert a plate over the pan and flip the omelet onto it. Slide the omelet back into the pan and brown the other side for a couple of minutes.

Ensalada (Spanish Salad)

2 heads romaine lettuce
2 stalks celery, chopped
2 large hardboiled eggs, peeled and chopped
2 ripe tomatoes cut into eight pieces
Manchego cheese shavings
¼ pound Serrano ham, sliced thin
1/3 cup Spanish olives, pitted

Dressing

1/8 cup sherry vinegar
3 cloves, garlic, grated
1 teaspoon Worcestershire sauce

1 teaspoon dried oregano
1 tablespoon fresh lemon juice
Kosher salt and pepper to taste
½ cup extra-virgin olive oil

Using a wire whisk, mix together the vinegar, garlic, Worcestershire, oregano, lemon juice, salt and pepper in a bowl. Gradually beat in olive oil to form an emulsion. When ready to serve, add your dressing to your salad, toss and enjoy with shavings of Manchego cheese and Serrano ham.

Chicken, Shrimp and Scallop Paella

One of my all-time favorite dishes is paella. Pieces of moist and flavorful chicken, shrimp and sea scallops cooked in Arborio rice make this a show-stopping entrée. Paella can be a pricey dish to make, so I only make it on very special occasions.

One summer my parents came to visit us in North Carolina. My Dad had just retired. I created this special dish for him in celebration. My dad accompanied me to the grocery store to purchase some of the ingredients I was missing. He was flabbergasted at the price of saffron—one of the most expensive spices in the world!

Later that month, an unexpected package appeared on our doorstep. Nestled in the large box were two large tins of saffron. I knew immediately that my parents had sent this package to me. My parents' generosity continually amazes me.

4 boneless, skinless chicken breasts, cut up into bite size pieces
¼ cup olive oil
Kosher salt and pepper to taste
8 ounces deveined shrimp without shells
1 large onion, chopped
¾ cup Portuguese chourico or Spanish sausage
4 cloves of garlic, minced
1 red bell pepper, seeded and chopped
1 green bell pepper, seeded and chopped
2 bay leaves—dried or fresh
1 teaspoon saffron
2 teaspoon thyme
1½ cups canned Italian tomatoes, drained and broken up with your hands
1½ cups Arborio rice
1 cup clam juice
1½ cups low-sodium chicken broth
12 large sea scallops, cut in quarters or ½ lb or so bay scallops
1 cup frozen peas
Lemon slices for garnish

Season the chicken breasts with salt and pepper. In a large Dutch oven or paella pan, sauté the breasts in olive oil until it's browned on all sides. Remove the browned chicken from the pan, place it on a platter and add in the deveined shrimp for about one minute, or until it's pink. Remove the shrimp from the pan and set it aside with chicken. Add in your onion, red bell pepper, and green bell pepper. Cook the vegetables for 10 minutes, stirring frequently. Add in the sliced chourico, minced garlic, bay leaves, saffron threads and thyme. Season the mixture with salt and pepper. Stir it for 1 minute. Add in the tomatoes and bring to a boil. Now, in goes the beautiful Arborio rice-- cook it until it's translucent. Add in the clam juice and low-sodium chicken stock to pan. Cover your pot or pan tightly and cook the paella for five minutes. Work in the chicken and shrimp and tuck in a dozen or so scallops and the peas. Cover the paella again and let it cook for 15 minutes more, or until most of the liquid is absorbed.

Garnish the dish with lemon slices. You're going to love this recipe! I can see it gracing your dinner table during special occasions, holidays, birthdays, and anniversaries!

Did you know?

Ever wonder why saffron is the world's most expensive spice? Saffron comes from the saffron crocus flower, which is native to Southwest Asia but grows abundantly in Spain. The actual saffron threads used in cooking are the flowers' stigma, or the delicate stalks that hold their pollen. What makes saffron so expensive is the intensive labor required to produce it. There are only 3 stigmas per flower, and it takes 80,000 flowers (or one whole acre) just to get one pound of saffron threads. The threads must be delicately harvested and dried by hand. Saffron's rich, complex flavor and the deep yellow-orange color it adds to food makes it worth the expense for a very special meal!

Spanish Flan (Custard)

Each time I make custard, my grandmother Vavo comes to mind. God bless her heart, Vavo had diabetes and a sweet tooth--not a good combination! Vavo's kitchen was located in the lower level of the three-tenement house. This was very convenient, as it kept her cool during the hot and humid New England summers. My grandmother often said that going up and down the basement stairs kept her nimble.

The cool basement was not only excellent for storing canned and dry goods, but it made a great hiding place for cookies, cakes, and especially custard pies--custard pies that my grandmother knew were off limits!

One ordinary weekday afternoon, my mother, sister and I stopped by Vavo's house on our way upstairs to our cozy apartment. As we entered we were startled by the sound of despondent weeping. Alarmed, we hurried down the stairs. There sat my dear grandmother at her kitchen table, her hands covering her face, crying uncontrollably. When we asked her what was wrong, she pointed to the corner of the kitchen and cried out "Look!" in her Portuguese accent. We looked, and there sat my beloved dog and best friend, Mademoiselle, happily licking sweet yellow custard from all over her face, neck and paws. The look of obvious joy on Mademoiselle's face stood in sharp contrast to Vavo's bereaved expression. Although we felt terrible for my grandmother, we all exploded in laughter! That'll teach you, Vavo! Good girl, Mademoiselle! Way to look out for Vavo while we're gone.

I enjoy teaching children how to make this Spanish dessert during my Kid's Culinary Adventure Summer Camps. Even students who THINK they will not like this dessert LOVE it! The soft, smooth and creamy texture of the custard is soothing, and the crunch of caramelized sugar on top adds the perfect touch of contrast to this incredible dessert.

Begin by making caramelized sugar.

Caramelized Sugar

1 cup granulated sugar
1 tablespoon water

Add the sugar and water to a small pan. Cook them over medium heat, stirring constantly until the sugar turns golden. Be attentive and watch because it will happen quickly. Once it changes color, pour it immediately into the bottom of six ovenproof ramekin cups.

Custard

2 cups milk
1 strip lemon peel
1 cinnamon stick
6 large eggs
6 tablespoons granulated sugar
1 teaspoon pure vanilla extract
Pinch of kosher salt

Boil the milk together with the lemon peel and cinnamon stick. In a large bowl, lightly beat the eggs with wire whisk. Blend in the sugar, vanilla, and salt. Gradually add the milk to your egg mixture and strain.

Pour the liquid into the ramekins filled with caramelized sugar. Place the ramekins in a pan of hot, two-inch deep water and bake it in a 300 degree F oven for 1 hour. Carefully remove the ramekins and cool them in the refrigerator.

Unmold your flan by running a knife around the edges. Invert onto a serving plate and enjoy!

ITALY

Farro with Cherry Tomato Salad with Goat Cheese and Lemon Pesto

Sausage Lentil Soup

Chicken Milanese

Cavatappi with Tomato and Garlic

Polenta-Cherry Cobbler

Like the Portuguese, Italians have a true zest for life and a warm, generous and lively spirit. And like the Portuguese, Italians love feeding people, and especially love feeding the hearts of their families through their stomachs! Both Italians and the Portuguese rely on the quality of ingredients rather than a highly involved or elaborate meal. I love the simplicity, honesty and richness of Italian food!

Farro and Cherry Tomato Salad with Goat Cheese and Lemon Pesto

Serves 6

Farro, or emmer wheat, has been cropping up all over the place lately, so hopefully you've heard of it. If not, it is a beautiful wheat grain–a kernel, really–that resembles barley. Whole grains are making a big comeback right now–quinoa, bulgur, etc., but farro is the only one that I really get excited about. It's chewy and slightly sweet and has a wonderful, nutty flavor. Farro can be used in salads, soups, risotto-inspired dishes, and about a million other things. Because Italians enjoy simple, rustic fare, farro makes a great complement to many Italian meals.

1¼ cups farro
1¼ teaspoons salt
3 cups water

Pesto

1 garlic clove
Zest from one lemon…Wait; don't throw that lemon out!
Juice of one lemon
¼ cup or so olive oil
1 cup basil leaves
1 cup fresh spinach leaves
Handful of fresh parsley
½ cup freshly grated parmesan

Salad

1/3 cup pine nuts, toasted
½ cup pitted Kalamata olives, halved
1 basket cherry tomatoes, halved
4 cups pre-washed baby spinach
2 ounces goat or feta cheese, crumbled

In a medium saucepan, combine the water with the farro. For added flavor you can substitute chicken or vegetable stock for the water. Bring the farro to a boil over high heat. Cover it and simmer it over medium-low heat until the farro is almost tender--about 20 minutes. Add in the salt and simmer until the farro is completely tender--about 10 minutes longer. Drain well. Transfer it to a large bowl and let cool.

To make your pesto, place all of the pesto ingredients in a food processor or blender and blend until they're smooth.

For the salad, place the pine nuts, olives, tomatoes and arugula in a large bowl with the farro. Add the pesto and toss to combine. Season your salad generously with salt and fresh cracked black pepper, and then top with goat cheese.

Tip: Using only basil in pesto can be pretty pricey, and if you're like me and grow herbs in your garden or in pots around your house, you don't want to take a whole bunch for just for one recipe. Supplementing the basil with fresh spinach leaves saves you money and adds layers of flavor and nutritional value! Your family should kiss you!

Sausage Lentil Soup

There's just something very comforting about a simmering pot of hearty, homemade soup.

Although I love cooking at home, my hubby and I enjoy a nice date night each week. Making time for each other has been vital for keeping our marriage healthy. One evening we decided to eat at one of our favorite Italian restaurants. We ordered a salad and a delicious soup with Italian sausage and lentils. My husband smiled as I carefully picked apart my soup. I was surveying all of the ingredients of course!

Unable to get the soup out of my mind, I experimented all week until I achieved the flavors I had enjoyed at the restaurant. I'm so happy I decided to develop this recipe, because it ended up being one of my son Alex's favorite soups.

1 pound Italian pork or turkey sausage
3 celery stalks (leaves included)
1 onion, quatered
4 cloves garlic, minced
3 carrots
1½ quarts water
4 to 5 tablespoons low-sodium chicken base or to taste
2 teaspoons dried oregano
1 tablespoon garlic powder
1 teaspoon dried basil
½ teaspoon ground black pepper
2 cups dried lentils, rinsed
1 bunch kale, cleaned and chopped

In a large soup pot, brown the crumbled sausage. Drain most of the fat and dry off the meat with paper towels. In a food processor, grate the celery, onion, garlic and carrots and add them to your soup pot. Add in the water, chicken base, dried oregano, garlic powder, dried basil, ground pepper, dried lentils and chopped kale. Bring the soup to a boil, lower the heat and let simmer for one and half hours, stirring occasionally. Being even better the next day, I try to make this soup the day before.

Chicken Milanese

It was a Sunday afternoon. October was upon us and the weather was calling us outdoors. Hours later, in need of a quick and flavorful dinner, I chose to make Chicken Milanese. This recipe was super-delicious, quick, and made the perfect Sunday dinner.

4 thin boneless chicken breasts
2 large eggs
1 tablespoon fresh lemon juice
1 cup Panko breadcrumbs
½ teaspoon Slap Ya Mama (or a mixture of garlic, onion powder, salt and cayenne)
1 tablespoon dried parsley
1 fresh tomato, sliced
4 slices provolone cheese
2 tablespoons salted butter
½ cup olive oil for frying

Place the chicken breasts between two sheets of plastic wrap and pound them thin with a mallet. A hammer, rolling pin or even a canned good from your pantry or cupboard will do in a pinch. I love buying chicken breasts that are already thin—it's a time and energy saver.

In a bowl, beat together the eggs and lemon juice.

On a plate, mix together the breadcrumbs, Slap Ya Mama seasoning, and parsley flakes.

Dip the flattened chicken into your egg mixture and then into seasoned Panko breadcrumbs. Place the breaded chicken on a plate and continue breading all other chicken breasts. (If you do not want to fry these up right away, you can refrigerate them).

Preheat your oven to 350 degrees. Heat the olive oil and butter in a frying pan and brown each chicken breast for about four minutes per side. Place the breasts in a baking dish and cover each piece with two slices of tomato and a slice of provolone cheese. Bake them in the oven until the tomato has softened and the cheese has melted.

Cavatappi with Tomatoes and Garlic

My husband and I adore the spiral tube shaped pasta known as cavatappi. Sauces of all sorts cling nicely to the texture of this pasta and the taste is delicious! This dish is not overpowered by sauce however and each ingredient shines. Like all pasta, be sure not to overcook the cavatappi because al dente is always best. This dish is perfect as a side dish or a satisfying main meal. And it couldn't be simpler to make!

4 tablespoons olive oil
4 tablespoons salted butter
1 pint cherry tomatoes
4 cloves garlic, peeled and smashed
4 sprigs thyme, stems on
1/4 teaspoon dried red crushed pepper
3 tablespoons fresh chiffonade of basil or 1 tablespoon Garden Gourmet basil herb blend
1 pound dried cavatappi pasta
1 tablespoon kosher salt for pasta water
Fresh Parmesan cheese, finely grated

In a large skillet, over medium-high heat, sauté the tomatoes, garlic, thyme, crushed red pepper flakes and basil in olive oil and butter. A small tip: use the thyme sprig as well as the leaves because the flavor is great. Cook the mixture for 15 minutes, stirring occasionally. Boil your cavatappi in well salted water until it's soft, yet still firm. When you're ready to serve your pasta, remove the thyme sprigs, add the cavatappi to the sauce, along with a little pasta water if necessary. Grate fresh Parmesan cheese over the pasta.

Polenta-Cherry Cobbler

I love any and all types of cobblers--especially those topped with fresh whipped cream or vanilla ice cream. I love the contrast of the cool cream with the warmth of the cobbler when it's right from the oven. This recipe should be titled DO NOT MIX cobbler! One of the easiest cobblers you'll ever make, this comforting recipe will please every member of your family!

½ cup salted butter
½ cup unbleached all-purpose flour
½ cup polenta or corn grits
1 cup granulated sugar
2 teaspoon baking powder
½ teaspoon kosher salt
1 cup milk
2 cans cherry pie filling, or your favorite pie filling (blueberry, apple…)
½ teaspoon freshly ground nutmeg
Zest of one orange

Preheat your oven to 350 degrees F. Place one unwrapped stick of butter in a 9 x 13-inch baking pan in the oven. Place your baking pan in the oven. Your butter will only take a couple of minutes to melt.

While your butter is melting, mix together flour, sugar, baking powder and salt in a mixing bowl.

Add the milk, mix well. Carefully remove the baking pan out of the oven. Pour your batter directly into pan. Once the ingredients are in the pan, DO NOT MIX THEM!

Dollop the pie filling all over the batter. RESIST MIXING THE FILLING!

Grate the nutmeg and orange zest on top.

Place the cobbler on the center rack of your oven and bake it for 40 to 45 minutes, or until lightly browned.

Serve the cobbler warm with vanilla ice cream or a dollop of freshly whipped cream! *Someone's going to kiss you for making this dessert, I promise!*

Notes and Memories

FRANCE

French food is known for being rich, beautiful and fancy. But it doesn't have to be stuffy or intimidating! Even some well-known classics are easier to prepare than you might think. So get into the kitchen, try these recipes out, and impress your family with your *savoir-faire*!

Crisp Pear and Blueberry Salad with Roquefort and Spiced Pecans

Coq au Vin

Potato Puree

Berry Clafouti

Crisp Pear and Blueberry Salad with Roquefort and Toasted Walnuts

Walnut oil gives this salad such a rich, woodsy flavor, and the addition of pear adds such a nice sweetness and texture. Always try to consider textures as you create recipes. Top your salad with toasted walnuts for more texture and flavor.

4 cups mixed greens
2 pears, peeled, cored, sliced, and sprinkled with a little lemon juice
1 cup fresh blueberries
1 tablespoon of walnut oil
2 tablespoons of canola or sunflower oil
1 tablespoon of red wine vinegar
1 tablespoon Dijon mustard
Salt and pepper to taste
Roquefort cheese, crumbled
1 cup walnuts, toasted

In a dry pan, toast your walnuts, stirring constantly for a couple of minutes. Nuts burn quickly—never step away from the stove while you're toasting nuts.

Wash and dry your lettuce well. In a bowl mix together the vinegar, a little salt and pepper, and whisk in the walnut and vegetable oil.

Place mixed greens on each plate, top with pear slices and blueberries. Drizzle the salad with your vinaigrette and adorn with a few toasted nuts.

Note: My Spiced Nuts (page 96) would make a wonderful addition to this salad as well.

Coq au Vin

Legend has it that the Gauls gave Julius Caesar's cook a tough old rooster as a tribute for conquering them. Caesar's cook made the best of the old rooster and served it back to the Gauls. However, it is more likely that Coq au Vin evolved as a local recipe in France.

½ pounds bacon, chopped
2 chicken breasts
2 chicken thighs
2 chicken legs
½ cup all-purpose flour
Kosher salt
Ground black pepper
2 cloves garlic, chopped
One box of frozen pearl onions or jar of pickled pearl onions, drained
2 cups button mushrooms, or your favorite wild mushroom (a combination would be nice)
3 carrots, cut in 2-inch pieces
1 bottle of good Burgundy wine (if you wouldn't drink it-don't use it)
2 cups chicken broth
5 sprigs fresh thyme
2 teaspoons Herbs de Provence
3 bay leaves
2 tablespoons softened butter
2 tablespoons all-purpose flour
Fresh parsley, chopped, for garnish

In a large, heavy skillet or Dutch oven, fry the bacon over medium heat until crisp.

Transfer the bacon to paper towels to drain. Coat your chicken pieces in flour, salt and pepper. Brown the chicken in bacon fat on both sides. Remember not to touch or move the chicken until it has browned. Remove the chicken from the heat and set it on a plate.

Add garlic, onions, mushrooms and carrots into the pan. Sauté the vegetables for 2 minutes to soften. Return the chicken and all its juices to the pan and stir in the wine and broth. Add the herbs. Cover the pan and simmer the chicken for 1 hour.

While the chicken is cooking, mix together the butter and flour. Be sure to incorporate these very well before putting them into the pan. You don't want to have lumps of flour in your sauce. You can use equal parts of water and flour instead of butter and flour, but the butter adds a lot of flavor!

Stir in the butter and flour mixture. Continue to simmer it for 15 minutes, allowing the sauce to thicken a bit.

Serve the sauce on a bed of pureed potatoes. Top with the reserved crumbled bacon and fresh parsley. All that's left is to enjoy!

Potato Puree

6 large Idaho of Yukon Gold potatoes, cut into uniformed cubes
Kosher salt
Ground white pepper
1 to 1 ½ cups heavy cream
1 stick of cold butter, cut into cubes
A Food mill

Place your potatoes in a large pot. Add in enough water to cover them and season the water generously with salt. Bring the potatoes to a boil and cook them until they're "fork tender." Drain them well.

Place the cream and butter into a small saucepan and heat it through. Pass the potatoes through your food mill or ricer into a large bowl. Add about 1/4 of the hot cream and butter. Stir vigorously until the ingredients are thoroughly combined. Repeat this process until all of the cream and butter is incorporated. Taste to check the seasoning; add salt and white pepper as needed. For an amazing meal, serve these potatoes with Coq au Vin.

Berry Clafouti

This berry recipe, also known as clafouti aux cerises, is the most well-known version of the traditional puffed French custard cake. In France, it is customary to serve clafouti with the cherry pits intact. For ease at the table, and to ensure dental safety, make sure to pit the cherries or forewarn your guests of the tradition. Beautiful raspberries and blackberries have been used in this recipe. Clafouti, one of the simplest French desserts, is considered a fancy ending to any great meal. Add a little dusting of powdered sugar and a dollop of homemade whipped cream and you're ready to impress!

1 tablespoon softened butter
1 cup whole milk
¼ cup heavy cream
3 large eggs
¼ cup granulated sugar
2 teaspoons vanilla extract
½ teaspoon almond extract
¼ teaspoon salt
Zest of one orange
2/3 cup all-purpose flour
Approximately 2 cups of raspberries and blackberries (dark cherries can be used as well)
1 tablespoon confectioners' sugar (powdered) for garnish
Whipped cream for garnish

Preheat an oven to 350 degrees F. Coat a 9 x 9-inch square baking dish or a 9-inch deep-dish pie round with the softened butter.

In a large bowl, whisk together the milk, cream, eggs, sugar, extracts and orange zest and whisk away! Next add in your flour and salt, whisking until the mixture forms a smooth, thin batter.

Spread 3/4 cup of the batter onto the bottom of the prepared baking dish and bake it for about 5 minutes. Watch the batter closely and remove it before it cooks through completely. It should just start to thicken and set. (This will insure that the berries will not move around or sink.)

Transfer the dish to a heatproof surface and arrange the berries over the hot batter. Carefully ladle the remaining batter over the berries. Bake for an additional 35-40 minutes, until a knife inserted in the center comes out clean.

Sprinkle the confectioners' sugar over the finished clafouti, add a dollop of homemade whipped cream and serve warm.

This recipe makes 8 servings. Cherries are the traditional fruit of choice, but I have even seen this made with Clementines – use your imagination!

Notes and Memories

Mediterranean and Middle Eastern Cuisine

Hummus with Toasted Pita Chips

Al Motubug

Tabouleh

Greek Salad

Chicken and Spinach Spanakopita

Baklava

Kourabiethes or Greek Wedding Cookies

Hummus with Toasted Pita Chips

Once when we lived in the beautiful mountains of Asheville, North Carolina, my parents and their friend Peachie came to visit us. During their visit, Peachie showed me how to make this wonderful recipe the Lebanese way and I've enjoyed experimenting with it ever since. A few years ago, my dear friends Rod and Joy asked me to cater their New Year's Eve Party. They tell me that this hummus recipe took center stage; everyone loved it! This recipe makes a fun, healthy and easy snack or lunch, and takes no time at all to prepare. Kids can help with ease, and they'll certainly enjoy creating their own versions of this healthy alternative to chips and salsa.

1 (14.5-ounce) can organic low sodium garbanzo beans, drained with liquid reserved
4 tablespoons Tahini (sesame paste)
1 teaspoon kosher salt
1 teaspoon garlic powder
3 tablespoons fresh lemon juice

Some folks prefer using olive oil and not the liquid in the can of beans, but Peachie taught me this trick. I do like to use the liquid in low-sodium organic beans only. You can use a combination of liquid and olive oil if you'd like. Olive oil is very good for you.

In a blender or food processor, combine all of the ingredients and blend them well. Add in a little liquid at a time—you can always add in liquid to dry hummus, but you can't take liquid out of hummus that's too wet. You may find that you don't need to use all of the liquid.

This hummus is delicious with fresh vegetables, crackers or toasted pita chips. Toasted pita chips are easy to make; simply cut Ezekiel bread (or your favorite type of pita bread) in eighths and separate the slices to make 16 pieces. Bake the bread in a 350 degree F oven for a couple of minutes. You can also spray with non-stick cooking spray and sprinkle dried herbs over top.

I like using Ezekiel pita bread, as it's made with sprouted grains, which adds optimum flavor and nutritional value. You can find Ezekiel pita bread in specialty whole food stores or online.

Al Motubug

Makes 10 servings

Within Saudi Arabia is the Rub al Khali, the driest dessert in the world. Al Motubug is easily prepared there because of its readily available ingredients. I stumbled upon this recipe while researching the cuisine of the Middle East and it was not only a big hit with my family, particularly my son Nate, but with all of my students in my Kid's Culinary Adventure Class!

Similar recipes like this one can be found all over the internet, so I cannot take credit for this recipe, however, I have adapted it. The original recipe calls for six layers of dough which we found to be too thick and so we use only one layer which we think is delicious!

6 cups unbleached all-purpose flour

1 teaspoon kosher salt

Water

2 bundles leeks (medium sized)

1 teaspoon ground black pepper

1½ pounds ground beef

1 teaspoon kosher salt

3 yellow onions (finely chopped)

2 large eggs, beaten

Egg Wash

1 teaspoon egg

1 teaspoon water

Sift the flour and salt in together, then add in the water a little at a time, mixing the dough until it becomes soft but pliable. Divide the dough into ten pieces and knead each piece well. Place the dough on a tray sprinkled with a little water, cover with a dish towel, and let it rise for at least one hour. Place the ground beef in a saucepan along with the chopped onion, black pepper and salt. Stir the mixture over medium heat until it's cooked through. Set the meat aside until it cools.

Add 2 beaten eggs to the beef. Chop the leeks and wash them several times through a strainer. Drain the leeks and put them on a paper towel until the excess water is absorbed. Add them to ground beef. Cover a piece of dough in flour, roll it out, and place it over the backs of your hands. Pull your hands apart gently and stretch the dough until it becomes quite thin. Lay the dough out on a flat surface. Place some of the beef and leek mixture in the center of the dough. Place a little bit of egg wash on the edge of the dough and fold it over to close it and create a pie. The egg wash will help the dough stick. Repeat these steps with the remaining dough pieces and meat mixture. Heat 3 tablespoons of oil in a frying pan or griddle. Fry each meat pie over medium heat until both sides are golden brown. Avoid crowding the pan, as it will bring down the temperature of the oil and cause the dough to become soggy.

Tabouleh

10 ounces water
4 ounces bulgur
½ teaspoon grated lemon zest
2 tablespoons lemon juice
2 tablespoons extra-virgin olive oil
1 clove garlic, minced
½ teaspoon both kosher salt and pepper
¼ teaspoon ground cumin
1 (19 ounce) can chickpeas, drained
3 plum tomatoes, diced
¼ cucumber, diced
Small bunch flat leaf parsley, chopped
1 tablespoon mint, chopped
1 tablespoon fresh chives, chopped

Bring the water to a boil, then add in the bulgur. Cover, reduce the heat to low and cook for ten minutes, or until the water has completely dissolved. Using a fork, scrape the bulgur into a large bowl. Allow it to cool.

In a large bowl, combine the lemon zest, lemon juice, oil, garlic, salt and pepper and ground cumin. Add your bulgur wheat. Stir in the chickpeas, tomatoes, cucumber, parsley, mint, and chives.

Greek Salad

One year our family chose to study Greece in preparation for our Annual International Night. Our dentist's wife, and mother, who were born in Greece, came to our home and taught us some of their beloved family recipes. They also loaned us slides of their trips to Greece, Grecian dolls, prayer beads and other family items to use for our Greek display. We very much appreciated their time and effort, and we made a photo album that included Greek recipes and pictures of our time with their family in the heart of our home –our kitchen.

Greek Salad

Combination of Romaine, Green, Red and Bibb lettuce
2 cucumbers, seeded and sliced
1 cup crumbled feta cheese
1 cup pitted Kalamata or black olives
3 Roma tomatoes, sliced
½ red onion, sliced
Pepperoncini peppers, sliced (optional)
Grind of black pepper

In a large salad bowl, layer torn lettuces, cucumber, feta cheese, olives, tomatoes, red onion and pepperoncini peppers. Chill until ready to serve. Dress salad with Greek Dressing and toss when ready to eat.

Greek Salad Dressing

¼ cup olive oil
¾ teaspoon garlic powder
1 teaspoon dried oregano
¾ teaspoon dried basil
½ teaspoon ground black pepper
½ teaspoon kosher salt
½ teaspoon onion powder
½ teaspoon Dijon-style mustard
1/3 cup red wine vinegar
Juice of one lemon
Handful fresh flat-leaf parsley, chopped

In a very large container, mix together the olive oil, garlic powder, oregano, basil, pepper, salt, onion powder, and Dijon-style mustard. Pour in the vinegar and lemon juice and mix them vigorously until they're well blended. Store the dressing—tightly--covered at room temperature.

Chicken and Spinach Spanakopita

4 large boneless chicken breasts, cut into bite size pieces
Salt and pepper to taste
¼ cup unsalted butter
4 tablespoons olive oil
1 yellow onion, chopped
4 cloves garlic, minced
1 large bag fresh spinach leaves or 2 (10 ounce) packages frozen spinach, thawed and drained
1 tablespoon finely chopped fresh dill or 2 teaspoons dried dill
¾ cup dry white wine
½ pound crumbled feta cheese
4 large eggs, beaten
12 sheets Phyllo dough
1 stick of butter or non-stick butter spray

In a sauté pan, heat the oil over medium heat. Add in the chicken, onion and garlic and cook them for 5 minutes, or until the chicken is nicely browned. Add in the spinach and dill.

Add in the white wine and simmer the mixture until the wine cooks down a bit. Transfer everything to a bowl and let it cool slightly. Add in the feta cheese. Add in a little more salt and pepper if necessary. Next add in the eggs, one at a time, stirring in between each addition.

Preheat your oven to 350 degrees F. Stack phyllo dough on your work surface. Phyllo can dry out very quickly. Cover the portion you haven't used yet with a towel or cloth to keep it moist.

Brush a 9 x 13-inch baking pan with melted butter. Place one sheet of phyllo in the pan and brush it with melted butter. Layer 4 more sheets over this one, brushing each with melted butter after laying it down. You can also spray phyllo with non-stick butter spray. Spread 1/3 of the chicken and spinach filling on top of the first 5 sheets of phyllo. Place five more sheets of Phyllo dough over the spinach mixture, one at a time, brushing each with melted butter. Continue layering the spinach mixture and phyllo dough in this way until all of the ingredients are used up, ending with a layer of 5 sheets of phyllo dough. Remember to brush the final top sheet with butter.

Bake the spanakopita until it's golden brown, which should take 50 to 60 minutes. Remove it from oven and let it stand for 10 minutes before cutting it.

Baklava

I have made this dessert made with walnuts and with pistachios. Both ways are very tasty!

1 (16-ounce) packages phyllo dough
1 pound chopped nuts
1 cup butter
1 teaspoon ground cinnamon
1 cup granulated sugar
1 cup water
1 teaspoon pure vanilla extract
½ cup raw honey

Preheat your oven to 350 degrees F. Butter the bottoms and sides of a glass 9 x 13 inch baking dish.

Chop the nuts, place in a bowl, add cinnamon and toss to coat. Set aside. Unroll your phyllo dough. Cover the phyllo with a cloth to keep from drying out as you work.

Layer 2 sheets of phyllo dough in your baking dish. Brush each sheet with melted butter after you lay it down. Sprinkle 2 to 3 tablespoons of nut mixture on top. Top with two more sheets of buttered dough and another layer of nuts. Continue layering the nuts and sheets of dough until you have 8 layers. The top layer should be a layer of phyllo dough about 6 to 8 sheets deep.

Using a sharp knife, cut the layers into diamond or square shapes all the way down to the bottom of the dish. Bake the baklava for about 50 minutes, or until it's golden and crisp.

Make your sauce while your baklava is baking. Boil the sugar and water until the sugar is melted. Add in the vanilla and honey. Simmer for about 20 minutes.

Remove the baklava from oven and immediately spoon sauce over it. Allow it to cool. Cut and serve each piece in individual cupcake papers. If (I can't imagine you will) have leftovers, Baklava freezes well.

Kourabiethes (Greek Celebration Cookies)

2 cups sifted all-purpose flour
½ teaspoon baking powder
1 cup salted butter, softened
¼ cup confectioners' sugar
1 large egg yolk
2 tablespoons good brandy
½ teaspoon vanilla extract
Confectioners' sugar for decoration

Sift flour with baking powder. Set aside.

Cream your butter. Gradually add the sugar and beat it in until the butter becomes fluffy. Add in the egg yolk, brandy and vanilla. Beat the butter again until it's very light.

Blend in the flour and mix the ingredients until they form a soft, smooth dough. Chill the dough for 30 minutes or until it can be handled and shaped easily.

Preheat your oven to 325 degrees F.

Shape level tablespoonfuls of dough and roll each one into a one-inch ball. Place balls 1 inch apart on ungreased cookie sheet. Bake them for 25-30 minutes or until they turn a light brown. Make sure not to brown them too much.

Lay a large piece of parchment paper on your counter. Remove your cookies from the oven, place on paper and liberally dust with powdered sugar! The parchment paper will make clean up so much easier for you. Place each cookie in tiny cupcake papers.

JAMAICA

Creamy Jamaican Squash Soup

Jerk Chicken Kabobs

Fried Plantains

Rice and Peas

Jamaican Cornmeal Pudding

      Due its tropical location in the beautiful Caribbean Sea, Jamaica is a very popular place to vacation. No matter what the weather's like where you are, you can add some breezy Caribbean fun to your next casual dinner party or family night by serving a delicious Jamaican meal. Play some reggae or island music, dress your home up with some fun beach décor, and serve some colorful tropical drinks. You're in for a day of fun and fantastic flavors!

Creamy Jamaican Squash Soup

The tart apple and the zest of orange and lemon add a pleasant surprise to this delightfully comforting soup.

½ pound bacon, chopped
1 yellow onion, chopped
3 ribs of celery, chopped
1 carrot, grated
3 cloves garlic, minced
1 teaspoon dried thyme (pressed between fingers to release the oil)
1 butternut squash, peeled, seeds removed, chopped
1 tart green apple, peeled, cored, chopped
3 cups low sodium organic chicken broth
1 cup water
Zest of one orange
Zest of one lemon
½ teaspoon each nutmeg, cinnamon, mace and ground ginger
¼ teaspoon cayenne
Salt and pepper to taste
Fresh chopped chives, optional garnish

Set a large soup pot over medium-high heat and cook your favorite bacon up until crispy. Using a slotted spoon, remove onto a plate and set aside. Leaving the bacon fat you rendered in the pan, add in the onion, celery, carrots, garlic and thyme and sauté them for 5 minutes, taking care to turn the heat down if the vegetables begin to brown.

Add in the squash, apple, broth, water, orange and lemon zest, nutmeg, cinnamon, mace, ginger, cayenne, salt and pepper. Bring everything to a boil. Cover the pot, turn the heat down to a simmer and cook the soup for 30 minutes, or until the squash and carrots have softened. Puree the whole thing together. Garnish the soup with your cooked bacon and chives and all there's left to do is to enjoy!

Vegetarian Version: Simply omit the bacon and cook up the veggies in 2 tablespoons butter. Substitute vegetable stock for chicken stock. Crispy croutons would make a nice garnish.

Jamaican Jerk Chicken Kabobs

6 boneless chicken breasts, skin removed
6 tablespoons vegetable, olive or grapeseed oil
Juice and zest of one lime
2 shallots, chopped
1 Scotch Bonnet without the seeds or Habanero pepper, roughly chopped (you can add additional peppers if you enjoy extra heat)
3 garlic cloves chopped
2 tablespoons fresh thyme or 1 tablespoon dried thyme
1 tablespoon minced peeled ginger
1 tablespoon packed dark brown sugar or molasses
2 teaspoons ground allspice
2 teaspoon ground cinnamon
1 teaspoon freshly ground nutmeg
1 teaspoon kosher salt
¼ teaspoon ground black pepper
2 tablespoons white vinegar

Scotch Bonnet and Habanero peppers are very hot and should be handled using gloves. Because the ingredients for the jerk marinade will be blended, there is no need to chop the ingredients finely.

Setting the chicken aside, place all of the ingredients in your blender and blend them until smooth. This is your marinade.

Rinse the chicken breasts under running water, then pat them dry with paper towels. Cut the chicken into 2-inch pieces, and then place it into a container. Be sure to clean your sink out after well after rinsing your chicken to avoid cross-contamination.

Pour your jerk marinade over your chicken, coat the chicken well and cover it. Place the chicken in your refrigerate to marinate overnight, or for at least 4 hours.

Place each piece of chicken on a skewer, using 3 to 4 pieces per skewer. If you use wooden skewers, be sure to soak them in water for 15 to 30 minutes before placing them on a hot grill. Grill the chicken until the juices run clear. Serve this chicken with steamed rice or a nice hearty salad and enjoy!

Fried Plantains

Fried plantains are a common treat throughout the Caribbean and Central America. Their balance of gooey, crispy and starchy sweetness make them the perfect accent for beans and rice, or for nearly any spicy, savory meal.

4 plantains (yellow or spotted brown)
Canola oil for frying
Kosher salt to taste

Take the plantains out of their sleeves and cut them at an angle into ¼ inch chips.

Fill a pan ½ inch up its side with oil. Fry the plantains gently over medium-high heat until they are golden brown on each side.

Transfer the plantains to a paper towel-lined plate to drain the grease. These sweet treats are best served hot and sprinkled with a touch of salt.

Jamaican Rice

1 (14.5-ounce) can kidney beans, drained
1 to 2 cloves garlic, chopped
1¼ cup unsweetened coconut milk
2¼ cups low sodium organic chicken stock (vegetable stock can be substituted for a vegetarian version)
1½ cups basmati rice
¼ teaspoon dried thyme
Three scallions, chopped
1 teaspoon kosher salt
¼ teaspoon ground black pepper

To make Jamaican rice, we use our rice steamer. We add everything into the steamer at once, cover it, and cook it according to the rice cooker directions.

If you do not have a rice cooker, combine all of the ingredients in a saucepan and bring them to a boil. Reduce the heat to low and simmer it for approximately 20 to 30 minutes, or until the liquid is absorbed and the rice is fully cooked.

Jamaican Cornmeal Pudding

I grew up loving my grandmother's Rice Pudding and thought that the Cornmeal Pudding would be a nice experiment. Boy, was I glad I attempted to make this. I topped this unique and delicious dessert with toasted coconut and nuts! The textures were simply fantastic. Always consider textures when cooking or baking!

1 tablespoon softened butter
3 cups golden cornmeal or polenta
¾ cup unbleached all purpose flour
2 ¼ cups packed brown sugar
5 cups thick coconut milk
1 tablespoon ground cinnamon
1 ½ teaspoons freshly ground nutmeg
½ teaspoon ground cloves
1½ teaspoon kosher salt
½ cup raisins
½ cup of the shredded coconut, toasted

Preheat your oven to 350 degrees F.

Grease a 9 x 13 inch baking dish with softened butter.

In a large bowl, sift together the flour, cornmeal and raisins. In another large bowl, blend together the brown sugar, coconut milk, cinnamon, nutmeg, cloves and salt. Add them to the cornmeal mixture, stirring out any lumps. Add to dry and mix well.

Pour your mixture into the prepared pan and bake for 50 to 60 minutes, or until its set.

Allow the pudding to cool and serve it with whipped cream topped off with toasted nuts and shredded coconut.

Notes and Memories

What I learned around the table...

Makes for one very happy life!

Thank God for each new morning, each new breath and each new challenge

Fill your heart with heaping spoonfuls of **Unconditional Love**

Fill your mind with an overflowing amount of **Gratitude**

Surround yourself with **Family** and genuinely **Good Friends**

Laugh hard and often

Stock up on **Quality Time** with loved ones and those in need

Bestow Kindness on others, even when you are struggling

Always **Accept** words of wisdom and help graciously

Fill your cup with **Faith**

Add a pound of **Patience**

Stir in the spirit of **Generosity**

Smile big as soon as you see your spouse and children each morning

Welcome everyone with the warmth of a smile…even when you're not feeling your best

Live like a blind man and **See Only a Person's Heart**

Know no strangers

Learn from those who have come before you

Listen more than you speak…I'm still practicing this one

Always be **Courteous** and **Caring** to others

Treat people **How You Wish to be Treated**

Do what you love and love what you do--**Wholeheartedly**

Always hold dear a **Forgiving** heart

Try not to judge another--**No one is Perfect**

LIVE each day as if it's your last

Leave a **LEGACY**

Combine all of these ingredients to live a life full of joy and without regrets! Practice one or two of them each day to make your world, your life and yourself better all the time!

The Benefits of a Well Organized Kitchen

You'll find it easier to cook more often if your kitchen is tidy and organized. Many people enjoy cooking, but feel less-than-motivated because their kitchen is--dare I say it--messy. I've been there!

I hope you find the following tips helpful in keeping the heart of your home clean and inviting:

1. **Keep your fridge clean.** Okay, I'll admit it, no matter how organized I try to be there have been those times when I find a moldy piece of cheese or a rotten cucumber in the back of our refrigerator. **Be sure to clean out your refrigerator once a week, preferably before grocery shopping.**

2. **Keep your spices in one place.** Don't you laugh, but I alphabetize mine. Okay, well, you can laugh, but it *does* make it so much easier to locate what I need quickly. You don't have to go so far as to alphabetize your spices. But do transfer your dried herbs and spices into uniformly sized plastic jars or tins with lids. Find a size that will fit neatly in your drawer or cabinet, and mark each jar so that you can easily identify each spice.

3. **Keep track of your spices.** We all have two or three of the same jar of spice in our cabinet. Which one is old and which is new? As spices age they lose their freshness and flavor. To be sure you're using the most recent jar—and to keep from buying unnecessary extra jars, **mark the date of purchase on each one when you bring them home.**

4. **Keep your pantry in order.** Clean out your pantry a couple of times a month. It's super easy to come home with a load of groceries and throw everything in different places.

Instead, make an effort to keep your pantry and cupboards organized and remove old items to make room for new ones. An organized, clean pantry will not only help you find what you're looking for, but will help you take note of what you're running out of as well.

5. **Practice product rotation.** Place new items in the back of your pantry and older items in the front. This is a good tip for your fridge, too!

6. **Be sure to only keep things you use often.** Get rid of items in your cabinets, pantry and refrigerator that haven't been used in some time. You probably won't ever use them. They're taking up precious space. Give unwanted dishes, cups, and small appliances away to a shelter or to someone who has a need.

7. **Clean your cabinets inside and out a few times a year.** As I clean my cabinets out, I look for chipped plates and cups, which are not just unsightly but dangerous to the mouth of an unsuspecting person. Why have these items taken up valuable cabinet space? I remove any questionable pieces and take note of anything I need to replace.

8. **Organize your cabinets in the most functional way possible.** I organize mine so that the dishes, glasses and flatware are stored in the cabinets closest to my dishwasher. My coffee mugs and tea cups are located near the corner of my kitchen where my coffee maker and stove is. Storing items that are used together or complement one another saves time and simplifies everything.

9. **Separate your nice dishes from your everyday dishes.** Keep your everyday dishes closest to you, within easy reach, and keep your china up higher. Do the same with your everyday cups and your fancier glasses.

10. **Keep cookware and cooking utensils in the handiest possible place.** I keep my pots and pans near my stove and my bakeware near my wall oven and warming drawer. I keep all of my measuring cups, spoons, cooking utensils and mixing bowls in my island, where I do most of my prep work.

11. **Organize your cookbooks.** My beloved cookbooks are arranged not by height, but by frequency of use. Because I have so many, I generally take a day each year to assess which cookbooks I haven't used in a while and then pass them along to someone else who might appreciate them.

12. **Keep your counters clean and uncluttered.** The only small kitchen appliance I leave out on my counter is my coffee maker which I use each morning. Even though I use my electric stand mixer and my food processor often I still store them away. I do, however, keep them in an easily accessible place.

13. **Clean your kitchen counters and sink before you go to bed.** No one likes to wake up to a messy kitchen. Your kitchen is the heart of your home and a clean kitchen is inviting!

14. **Clean your appliances after each use**. Once they're clean, put each back in its special place.

15. **Group pantry items together.** Place cereals and breakfast items together. Coffee, tea and other beverages should be in one spot. All of my baking ingredients are grouped together, as are my pasta and rice containers and my oils and vinegars. Consider buying containers to store items like cereal and grains —they will keep your pantry looking more uniform and organized. Plus, they'll stay fresh for a longer period of time when stored in plastic or glass containers.

16. **Make the most of your freezer.** Set aside space (or utilize extra space) to keep items like flour, grains and coffee fresh.

17. **Keep your storage containers under control.** To avoid a mess, I keep all of my storage containers in a large, deep drawer, nestled together from large to small. I keep the lids separate, but easily accessible in a long container that keeps them corralled and easily identifiable.

18. **Designate a space for your dish towels.** I keep my collection of oven mitts and beloved dish cloths and dish towels in a large drawer. I love my dish towel collection! It just makes me happy. To keep my dish towels organized, I simply fold them in thirds (the long way) and then in half to form nice little squares that fit nicely in my drawer. Every once and a while, I get rid of towels that have served me well, but are past their prime. Then I have a handy excuse to buy another!

19. **Create a first aid/medicine storage area.** A couple of years ago, I purchased inexpensive plastic containers to hold first aid products, vitamins, skin care items, sunscreen and medicines. Each container is labeled and now all of the items can be found easily when needed. Always place first aid items, medications, and cleaning supplies in higher places to protect your little ones.

20. **Keep a calendar handy (and use it!).** I keep a large calendar in my pantry, which is near my phone and easily accessible. Because I often find myself in the pantry, I can always see what appointments are coming up and which errands need to be run. Keep your calendar in a highly visible place that you pass by often. In addition, keeping it near the phone is convenient for setting appointments and dates.

21. **Take charge of your junk drawer.** Everyone has a junk drawer—and good grief, they don't call it a junk drawer for nothing! Mine gets out of control if I don't stay on top of it. The key is organization. Use dividers to keep pens and pencils, scissors, tape, paper clips and glue organized. Wrap loose pens and pencils together with rubber bands. Keep your coupons in a binder, a photo album or coupon book—whatever fits your budget and needs. Check the dates regularly and get rid of any that have expired. Last but not least—go through your junk drawer regularly and throw out any junk that is no longer needed.

22. **Make the most of your cabinet space.** If you are like me, you have cabinets that you can hardly reach without a ladder or step stool! Hey, I'm only 5'2"! Use high cabinets for things that you don't use often, like cake plates or special holiday items.

23. **Set aside a space for gift wrapping items.** I store my wrapping paper, bags, ribbon, bows, tags, and other gift items in my laundry room cabinets, which are right by my kitchen. It's all in one place and ready when I need something. I like to save money by reusing gift bags and tissue paper in good condition. Did you know that reused tissue paper can look like new if ironed on a low setting? I do it all the time!

24. **Keeping the plastic grocery store bags** is a good idea if you don't have a garbage disposal. Tying up discarded food items before placing them in the trash will prevent the

kitchen from smelling. I always clean out my trash can before placing a new trash bag inside.

25. **Create storage when necessary.** If you don't have room to store all of your kitchen utensils in a drawer, for example, place an attractive container on the counter. Store what you use most frequently on the counter and store what you use less frequently in your drawer.

26. **Label everything for easy access and easy identification.** A label maker is a beautiful thing!

27. **Keep things stylish.** This is so important! Organize your kitchen according to how you like it. I like things neat and tidy and I keep my counters fairly uncluttered. Other people enjoy adding pretty things to their counters, or having their colorful utensils, silverware and glasses in plain sight. Anything that brings you joy in your kitchen and makes the heart of your home a wonderful place to spend time in is a great thing!

Helpful Meal Planning and Money Saving Tips

Planning a food budget is one of the most important things you can do to save money. With a food budget you are less likely to overspend and run out of food. Having a weekly menu will help keep you from stopping at the grocery store to find something for dinner. An unplanned trip to the grocery store, especially when you're hungry and in a hurry, will lead to a disaster! Think about how much it costs each month to feed your family. Set a number in your mind and see if you can stick to it. You may have to be flexible, but try sticking to the number you feel is attainable. Use the steps below to help you!

1. Buy on **sale** and in **bulk**!

2. **Staples** are foods that help you avoid having a bare cupboard, and last a long time. These might include peanut butter, flour, corn meal, sugar, dry milk, dry or canned beans, tuna, rice, pasta, spices, and salt.

3. **Watch the ads** and buy these staples in bulk when they're on sale. Your cupboard will always be full and you're now ready to move onto the next step! **Check the ads for sales** -- if you are almost out of something and it is on sale, put it on your list! Looking through supermarket ads will also give you some ideas about what you might like to cook that week.

4. **Buy in season** because certain items cost less when "in season" -- for example, zucchini might be $1.39 per pound in the winter and only $0.79 per pound in late summer.

5. **Check to see what you already have** -- be sure to look in your cupboards, your freezer, and your refrigerator. Keep plenty of staples on hand -- they store well, and stretch meals. "Staples" are also called "just in case foods."

6. **Canned tomatoes, tomato sauce, canned vegetables** (watch for corn syrup), jarred spaghetti sauce, raisins, canned or dry fruit, canned clams, canned and dry beans, peanut, almond and cashew butters and canned soups are **great staples**.

7. **Taking inventory** of what you have on hand will keep you from buying food you don't need. Use this inventory to decide your **weekly menu**.

8. Support your local farmers and their families who work so very hard by shopping at your **local Farmer's Market**. There you will find very fresh, local produce at an excellent price. It's also a nice way to get to know where your food comes from and who's caring for it!

9. Once you've checked the ads and looked at your staples, make a **weekly list** of meals. Make sure to look at your calendar to see how much time you have each day and plan accordingly. Using the staples and the ads will help you plan for the week and will also keep your list down and money in your pocket.

10. **Avoid grocery shopping when you're hungry**. Impulsive buying will cost you! Try not to go into the store for, what I call, the $50 gallon of milk. How many times have we entered the grocery store just for a gallon of milk and come out with three bags of unneeded groceries? Happens to the best of us!

11. It helps to keep a **notepad on the refrigerator** or in a drawer -- that way, when you run out of something during the week, you can write it down before you forget. If you're ready

to prepare a meal that you planned, but don't have that one ingredient you might be less apt to cook that night and resort to take out or a restaurant, ultimately costing you more money, so be sure you write it down right away!

12. **Choose items that are healthy for your family**. This will save you money in the end. You are what you eat! If you feed your family junk and processed foods, which seem to be cheaper, you'll end up having more doctor bills!

13. Your shopping list is **your "PLAN" for the week** -- and your job is to **STICK TO THE PLAN!**

14. It is very easy to come home with foods that aren't in your food budget. Grocery stores work hard to **get you to buy more than you planned**. We covered approaches you can take at home to stretch your food dollars. Now, let's look at strategies you can use at the grocery store.

15. **Grab** the item **and GO**! If you absolutely have to stop at the grocery store, leave the cart at the door.

16. Ever wonder what the **difference is between the "name" brand and the generic brand** of a food? Usually, only dollars and cents!

17. Companies spend a lot of money on advertising to get you to buy their brand -- but they aren't spending their money, they are **spending your money**.

18. The store brand or **generic brand almost always costs less**, and usually tastes the same. In fact, they often use the very same ingredients.

19. Try doing **a "blind" taste-test** with your kids: buy a generic and a name-brand box of the same cereal; pour two bowls, and don't tell them which one is generic -- see if they can guess the difference.

20. **Cereal is very expensive.** If you do purchase cereal, try buying one with a good amount of protein and fiber. This will keep your family more satisfied. Try making homemade oatmeal, muffins, pancakes and eggs. All these are healthier alternatives and will be **less costly**.

21. The **"unit price"** of a food is the price per pound or per ounce. When comparing the cost of two different sizes of the same food, or two different brands that are of different weights, it can be hard to figure out which one is a better buy. The tag on the shelf should tell you the total price and the unit price -- this way, you can get the best deal.

22. You will find that often the **bigger package is cheaper**. Even though you pay more up front for the larger size, you are getting a cheaper price on the whole.

23. **Hidden Persuaders** can get us to spend more money than we have on things we didn't plan to buy. Here are some hidden persuaders to look out for.

24. **Time**: the more time you spend in the store, the more money you spend. It helps to stick to your list!

25. **Shelf level and position**: foods at eye-level are more expensive -- this means your eyes and your children's eyes!

26. **Temptations -- samples**: it is fun to sample new food, but often these are expensive convenience foods, and very rarely are they generic brands or sale items.

27. **Convenience** -- There are so many **"ready-to-eat" foods** available, and boy, are they ever tempting! Keep in mind that making it yourself will almost always cost less, and will be much healthier for your family.

28. **Coupons** -- Clipping coupons can save you money -- but remember, coupons are usually for name brands. Even with a coupon (or sometimes double coupons!) the generic brand can sometimes cost less. You have to do a little math, but it is well worth the time.

29. **Shop at wholesale clubs** that encourage customers to use both in-store coupons and manufactures coupons.

30. **Reading labels** is a great way to make sure you get the best nutrition for your dollar. By looking at the "Nutrition Facts" label, you can watch your intake of fats and sugar, and compare amounts of nutrients like fiber, iron, and calcium.

31. Foods that have a **Nutrition Facts label** will also have an "ingredients" list. The ingredients are listed from "most" to "least" -- in other words, if corn syrup is the first ingredient, you know that the food is made mostly of corn syrup! It is good to check the ingredients list of foods like cereal and juice, and other foods that often contain added sugar.

32. **Whole foods** like fruits, vegetables, whole grains and legumes usually have no added fat or added sugar.

33. **Be flexible** -- if you see an unadvertised special that is too good to pass up, change your plan -- add that food to your list. Sometimes grocers need to make room and mark staple items down for quick sale. Other times, perishable foods like meat, milk, or produce are marked down for quick sale. Be sure to use these up quickly or freeze, and throw away anything that smells or tastes bad.

Index

A

A Medieval Murder Mystery Dinner, 78

Afternoon Tea
    Mom's Chicken Salad Sandwiches, 115
    Pumpkin Chip Scones, 122
    Pumpkin Spice Muffins, 121
    Roasted Asparagus Quiche, 116
    Strawberries and Cream Scones, 119
    Traditional Irish Scones, 197

Almond Cookies, 111

Appetizers
    Chicken and Vegetable Egg Rolls, 105
    Fresh Lettuce Wraps, 104
    Steamed Dumplings, 103

Apples
    Wholegrain Apple Oat Pancakes, 91

Arroz Doce (Rice Pudding), 84

Asparagus
    Asparagus, Potato and Onion Omelet, 199
    Roasted Asparagus Quiche, 116

Asparagus, Potato and Onion Omelet, 199

Award-Winning Recipes
    Chicken Tikka Masala, 181
    Naan Bread, 180
    Sing a Song of Sixpence French Meat Pie, 82
    Wholegrain Pan Rolls, 69

B

Back in the Day Wedge Salad with Thousand Island Dressing, 129

Baked Cheeseburger Macaroni, Please, 130

Baklava, 225

Bars
    Chocolate Peanut Butter Oat Bars, 35
    Oatmeal Chocolate Chip Cream Cheese Bars, 34
    Pecan Bars, 146

Basic Pizza Dough, 20

Beans
    Hummus, 219
    Jamaican Rice, 230
    Party Beans, 143
    Sausage Lentil Soup, 208

Beef
    Baked Cheeseburger Macaroni, Please!, 130
    Cottage Pie with Onion Gravy, 187
    Golabki (Stuffed Cabbage Rolls), 131
    Irish Beef Stew, 195
    Jamaican Jerk Chicken Kabobs, 229
    Mom's Portuguese Style Oven Roast, 72
    Sing a Song of Sixpence French Meat Pie, 82
    Sloppy Joe Sliders, 30
    Vavo's Spaghetti and Meatballs, 170
    Warm and Hearty Minestrone Soup, 45

Berries
    Berry Clafouti, 216
    Berry Parfaits, 125

Berry Clafouti, 216

Berry Parfaits, 125

Blueberries

    Blueberry Peach Crumb Cake, 198

    Crisp Pear and Blueberry Salad with Roquefort and Roquefort and Roquefort and Toast Walnuts, 213

Blueberry Orange and White Chocolate Buttermilk Pancakes, 92

Blueberry Peach Crumb Cake, 198

Breads

    Folar da Pascoa (Easter Bread), 177

    Herb Buttermilk Biscuits, 80

    Irish Soda Bread, 194

    Maple-Wheat Cloverleaf Rolls, 42

    Massa Sovado (Portuguese Sweet Bread), 175

    Naan Bread, 180

    Pumpkin Chip Scones, 122

    Pumpkin Spice Muffins, 121

    Rustic Brown Bread, 186

    Strawberries and Cream Scones, 119

    Toasted Pita Chips, 219

    Traditional Irish Scones, 197

    Wholegrain Pan Rolls, 69

Breakfast

    Asparagus, Potato and Onion Omelet, 199

    Pumpkin Granola Pancakes, 89

    Roasted Asparagus Quiche, 116

Breakfast Pizza, 23

Breakfasts

    Blueberry Buttermilk Pancakes, 92

    Breakfast Pizza, 23

    Cannoli filling, 94

    Cinnamon Roll Pancakes, 98

    Homemade Whipped Cream, 88

    Mock Maple Syrup, 88

    Orange Maple Syrup, 93

    Sweet Potato Pancakes adorned with Spiced Nuts, 96

    Wholegrain Apple Oat Pancakes, 91

Brunch

    Asparagus, Potato and Onion Omelet, 199

    Berry Parfaits, 125

    Mom's Chicken Salad Sandwiches, 115

    Pumpkin Chip Scones, 122

    Pumpkin Spice Muffins, 121

    Roasted Asparagus Quiche, 116

    Strawberries and Cream Scones, 119

    Traditional Irish Scones, 197

Burgers

    Spinach Feta Turkey Burgers with Green Goddess Mayo, 141

Butternut Squash

    Creamy Jamaican Squash Soup, 228

C

Cabbage

    Golabki (Stuffed Cabbage Rolls), 131

Caesar's Tableside Salad, 52

Cakes

    Blueberry Peach Crumb Cake, 198

    Green Tomato Spice Cake with Brown, 75

    Hawaiian Cake, 145

    Jamaican Cornmeal Pudding, 231

    The Generations Cake, 153

Cannoli filling, 94

Carrot

    Spread the Love Spiced Carrot Marmalade, 43

Carrot Potato Mash, 74

Carrots

    Carrot Potato Mash, 74

    The Generations Cake, 153

Casseroles

    Baked Cheeseburger Macaroni, Please!, 130

Cottage Pie with Onion Gravy, 187
Golabki (Stuffed Cabbage Rolls), 131

Cavatappi
Cavatappi with Tomatoes and Garlic, 210

Cavatappi with Tomatoes and Garlic, 210

Cheese
Baked Cheeseburger Macaroni, Please!, 130
Crisp Pear and Blueberry Salad with Roquef, 213

Cherries
Polenta-Cherry Cobbler, 211

Chicken
Chicken and Spinach Spanakopita, 224
Chicken and Vegetable Egg Rolls, 105
Chicken Fried Rice, 109
Chicken Milanese, 209
Chicken Tikka Masala, 181
Chicken, Shrimp and Scallop Paella, 201
Coq au Vin, 214
Grilled Lemon Chicken, 142
Jamaican Jerk Chicken Kabobs, 229
Klingon "Heart of Tagh" or Sesame Chicken, 152
Mom's Chicken Salad Sandwiches, 115

Chicken and Spinach Spanakopita, 224

Chicken and Vegetable Egg Rolls, 105

Chicken Fried Rice, 109

Chicken Milanese, 209

Chicken Tikka Masala, 181

Chicken, Shrimp and Scallop Paella, 201

Chinese Recipes
Almond Cookies, 111
Chicken and Vegetable Egg Rolls, 105
Chicken Fried Rice, 109
Fortune Cookies, 110
Nate's Delicious Dipping Sauce, 103
Steamed Dumplings, 103

Chocolate
Chocolate Wine Sauce, 94
Double Peanut Butter Chocolate, 46
Heavenly Chocolate Pudding, 136
Pumpkin Chip Scones, 122

Chocolate Peanut Butter Oat Bars, 35

Chocolate Wine Sauce, 94

Cinnamon Roll Pancakes, 98

Coconut
Hawaiian Cake, 145
Jamaican Cornmeal Pudding, 231
Jamaican Rice, 230

Colcannon, 196

Compound Butters, 70
Chive Butter, 71
Cinnamon Butter, 71
Garlic Butter, 71
Herb Butter, 70
Lemon or Lime Butter, 71
Peach, Raspberry or Strawberry Butter, 71

COOKIE BAKING TIPS, 38

Cookies
Almond Cookies, 111
COOKIE BAKING TIPS, 38
Cranberry and White Chocolate Biscotti, 63
Double Peanut Butter Chocolate, 46
Fortune Cookies, 110
Kourabiethes (Greek Celebration Celebration Cookies), 226
Orange Vanilla Sugar Cookies, 37

Coq au Vin, 214

Cottage Pie with Onion Gravy, 187

Cranberry and White Chocolate Biscotti, 63

Creamed Corn, 134

Creamy Jamaican Squash Soup, 228

Creamy Potato Leek Soup, 81

Crepes
Cannoli filling, 94

Crisp Pear and Blueberry Salad with Roquefort and Toasted Walnuts, 213

Cucumber

    Raita, a Cool Cucumber Yogurt Sauce, 184

Curry Sauce, 182

D

Desserts

    Arroz Doce (Rice Pudding), 84

    Baklava, 225

    Berry Clafouti, 216

    Berry Parfaits, 125

    Blueberry Peach Crumb Cake, 198

    Cannoli filling, 94

    Chocolate Peanut Butter Oat Bars, 35

    Chocolate Wine Sauce, 94

    Cinnamon Roll Pancakes, 98

    COOKIE BAKING TIPS, 38

    Cranberry and White Chocolate Biscotti, 63

    Double Flaky Pie Crust, 82

    Double Peanut Butter Chocolate, 46

    English Bread Pudding with Caramel Sauce, 190

    Fortune Cookies, 110

    Green Tomato Spice Cake with Brown, 75

    Hawaiian Cake, 145

    Heavenly Chocolate Pudding, 136

    Homemade Whipped Cream, 88

    Jamaican Cornmeal Pudding, 231

    Kourabiethes (Greek Celebration Celebration Cookies), 226

    Lavender Almond Panna Cotta with, 64

    Malasadas (Portuguese Fried Dough, 173

    Mock Maple Syrup, 88

    Oatmeal Chocolate Chip Cream Cheese Bars, 34

    Orange Maple Syrup, 93

    Orange Vanilla Sugar Cookies, 37

    Peanut Butter Milkshakes, 135

    Pecan Bars, 146

    Polenta-Cherry Cobbler, 211

    Spanish Flan (Custard), 202

    Spice Glaze, 122

    Strawberries and Cream Scones, 119

    The Generations Cake, 153

Dinner

    Asparagus, Potato and Onion Omelet, 199

Double Flaky Pie Crust, 82

Double Peanut Butter Chocolate S'mores, 46

Drinks

    Hot Cocoa with Peppermint Whipped Cream, 41

    Peanut Butter Milkshakes, 135

    Romulan Ale, 151

    Southern Sweet Tea with a Twist, 47

E

Easter

    Folar da Pascoa (Easter Bread), 177

Egg Rolls

    Tips for Making Egg Rolls, 106

Eggs

    Asparagus, Potato and Onion Omelet, 199

    Roasted Asparagus Quiche, 116

    Spanish Flan (Custard), 202

English Bread Pudding with Caramel Sauce, 190

English Recipes

    Blueberry Peach Crumb Cake, 198

    Cottage Pie with Onion Gravy, 187

    English Bread Pudding with Caramel Sauce, 190

    Mushy Peas, 189

    Rustic Brown Bread, 186

Ensalada (Spanish Salad), 200

F

Fall River, Massachusetts

Heavenly Chocolate Pudding, 136

Malasadas, 173

Massa Sovado (Portuguese Sweet Bread), 175

Mom's Baked Pork Chops, 134

Mom's Chicken Salad Sandwiches, 115

Mom's Portuguese Style Oven Roast, 72

My Grandmother's Sour Soup (Caldo Azedo), 72

My Grandmother's Spaghetti Sauce, 172

Portuguese Kale Soup, 164

Portuguese Stuffing, 168

Vavo's Spaghetti and Meatballs, 170

Fish

Vavo's Pan Fried Fish and Red Gravy with Stewed Potatoes, 165

Folar da Pascoa (Easter Bread), 177

Fortune Cookies, 110

French Recipes

Berry Clafouti, 216

Coq au Vin, 214

Crisp Pear and Blueberry Salad with Roquefort and Roquefort and Roquefort and Toast Walnuts, 213

Fresh from the Garden Pizza Sauce, 21

Fried Plantains, 230

Fruit

Berry Clafouti, 216

Crisp Pear and Blueberry Salad with Roquefort and Roquefort and Roquefort and Toast Walnuts, 213

G

Garlic

Cavatappi with Tomatoes and Garlic, 210

My Garlic Mashed Potatoes, 187

***Get Me a Man* Pie, 138**

Glazes

Spice Glaze, 122

Golabki (Stuffed Cabbage Rolls), 131

Granny's Pineapple Cake, 156

Granola

Pumpkin Granola Pancakes, 89

Granola Clusters, 48

Gravies

Onion Gravy, 187

Red Gravy, 165

Greek Recipes

Baklava, 225

Chicken and Spinach Spanakopita, 224

Greek Salad, 223

Kourabiethes (Greek Celebration Celebration Cookies), 226

Greek Salad, 222

Green Tomato Spice Cake with Brown Butter Icing, 75

Green Tomatoes

Green Tomato Spice Cake with Brown, 75

Grilled Lemon Chicken, 142

Grilling

Grilled Lemon Chicken, 142

Spinach Feta Turkey Burgers with Green Goddess Mayo, 141

H

Hawaiian Cake, 145

Heavenly Chocolate Pudding, 136

Helpful Meal Planning and Money Saving Tips, 241

Herb Buttermilk Biscuits, 80

Homemade Fettuccini with Bolognese Sauce, 53

Homemade Whipped Cream, 88

Hot Cocoa with Peppermint Whipped Cream, 41

Hummus, 219

I

Ice Cream
    Peanut Butter Milkshakes, 135
Indian Recipes
    Chicken Tikka Masala, 181
    Curry Sauce, 182
    Infused Basmati Rice, 183
    Naan Bread, 180
    Raita, a Cool Cucumber Yogurt Sauce, 184
Infused Basmati Rice, 183
Irish Beef Stew, 195
Irish Recipes
    Colcannon, 196
    Irish Beef Stew, 195
    Irish Soda Bread, 194
    Traditional Irish Scones, 197
Irish Soda Bread, 194
Italian Recipes
    Cavatappi with Tomatoes and Garlic, 210
    Chicken Milanese, 209
    Polenta-Cherry Cobbler, 211
    Sausage Lentil Soup, 208

J

Jamaican Cornmeal Pudding, 231
Jamaican Jerk Chicken Kabobs, 229
Jamaican Recipes
    Creamy Jamaican Squash Soup, 228
    Fried Plantains, 230
    Jamaican Cornmeal Pudding, 231
    Jamaican Jerk Chicken Kabobs, 229
    Jamaican Rice, 230
Jamaican Rice, 230

K

Kale
    Colcannon, 196
    Portuguese Kale Soup, 164
    Sausage Lentil Soup, 208
Klingon "Gagh" or Noodles in Peanut Sauce, 152
Klingon "Heart of Tagh" or Sesame Chicken, 152
Kourabiethes (Greek Celebration Cookies), 226

L

Lavender Almond Panna Cotta with Roasted Cherries, 64
Lemon
    Grilled Lemon Chicken, 142
Lentils
    Sausage Lentil Soup, 208
Lunch
    Mom's Chicken Salad Sandwiches, 115
    Roasted Asparagus Quiche, 116

M

Main Dishes
    Breakfast Pizza, 23
    Chicken Fried Rice, 109
    Chicken Milanese, 209
    Chicken Tikka Masala, 181
    Chicken, Shrimp and Scallop Paella, 201
    Coq au Vin, 214
    Cottage Pie with Onion Gravy, 187
    Creamy Potato Leek Soup, 81
    Golabki (Stuffed Cabbage Rolls), 131
    Grilled Lemon Chicken, 142
    Homemade Fettuccini with Bolognese Sauce, 53
    Irish Beef Stew, 195
    Jamaican Jerk Chicken Kabobs, 229

Klingon "Heart of Tagh" or Sesame Chicken, 152
Mediterranean Pizza, 23
Mom's Baked Pork Chops, 134
Mom's Portuguese Style Oven Roast, 72
My Grandmother's Sour Soup (Caldo Azedo), 72
My Grandmother's Spaghetti Sauce, 172
Portuguese Kale Soup, 164
Roasted Asparagus Quiche, 116
Roasted Vegetable Lasagna, 56
Sausage and Pepper Heros, 31
Sausage Lentil Soup, 208
Sausage Ravioli with Brown Butter Sauce, 60
Sing a Song of Sixpence French Meat Pie, 82
Sloppy Joe Sliders, 30
Spaghetti with Spicy Sausage and Pepper Sauce, 59
Vavo's Pan Fried Fish and Red Gravy with Stewed Potatoes, 165
Vavo's Spaghetti and Meatballs, 170
Warm and Hearty Minestrone Soup, 45

Make-Your-Own-Pizza Night, 25

Malasadas

Malasadas (Portuguese Fried Dough, 173

Malasadas (Portuguese Fried Doughnuts), 173

Mamma's Pecan Pie, 148

Maple-Wheat Cloverleaf Rolls, 42

Massa Sovado (Portuguese Sweet Bread), 175

Mediterennean Recipes

Greek Salad, 222
Hummus, 219
Tabouleh, 222
Toasted Pita Chips, 219

Mediterranean Pizza, 23

Middle Eastern Recipes

Hummus, 219
Tabouleh, 222
Toasted Pita Chips, 219

Mock Maple Syrup, 88

Mom's Baked Pork Chops, 134

Mom's Chicken Salad Sandwiches, 115

Mom's Portuguese Style Oven Roast, 72

Mom's Recipes

Mom's Chicken Salad Sandwiches, 115
Mom's Portuguese Style Oven Roast, 72

Mom's Chicken Salad Sandwiches

Sandwiches, 115

Mom's Recipes

Mom's Baked Pork Chops, 134

Muffins

Pumpkin Spice Muffins, 121

Multigrain Pizza Dough, 20

Mushrooms

Coq au Vin, 214

Mushy Peas, 189

My Garlic Mashed Potatoes, 187

My Grandmother

Folar da Pascoa (Easter Bread), 177
Heavenly Chocolate Pudding, 136
Malasadas (Portuguese Fried Dough, 173
Massa Sovado (Portuguese Sweet Bread), 175
My Grandmother's Sour Soup (Caldo Azedo), 72
My Grandmother's Spaghetti Sauce, 172
Portuguese Kale Soup, 164
Portuguese Stuffing, 168
Vavo's Pan Fried Fish and Red Gravy with Stewed Potatoes, 165
Vavo's Spaghetti and Meatballs, 170

My Grandmother's Sour Soup (Caldo Azedo), 72

My Grandmother's Spaghetti Sauce, 172

N

Naan Bread, 180

Nate's Delicious Dipping Sauce, 103

Tortellini Salad, 143

Nuts
    Baklava, 225
    Crisp Pear and Blueberry Salad with Roquefort and Roquefort and Roquefort and Toast Walnuts, 213
    Sweet Potato Pancakes adorned with Spiced Nuts, 96

O

Oatmeal Chocolate Chip Cream Cheese Bars, 34
Old Faithful Whipped Mashed Potatoes, 133
Orange Maple Syrup, 93
Orange Vanilla Sugar Cookies, 37

P

Pancakes
    Blueberry Buttermilk Pancakes, 92
    Cinnamon Roll Pancakes, 98
    Mock Maple Syrup, 88
    Pumpkin Granola Pancakes, 89
    Sweet Potato Pancakes adorned with Spiced Nuts, 96
    Wholegrain Apple Oat Pancakes, 91

Party Beans, 143

Party Favorites
    Mom's Chicken Salad Sandwiches, 115

Party Recipes
    Chicken, Shrimp and Scallop Paella, 201
    Klingon "Gagh" or Noodles in Peanut Sauce, 152
    Klingon "Heart of Tagh" or Sesame Chicken, 152
    Tortellini Salad, 143
    Party Beans, 143
    Roasted Asparagus Quiche, 116
    Romulan Ale, 151
    Summer Potato Salad, 144
    The Generations Cake, 153

Pasta
    Cavatappi with Tomatoes and Garlic, 210
    Homemade Fettuccini with Bolognese, 53
    Klingon "Gagh" or Noodles in Peanut Sauce, 152
    My Grandmother's Spaghetti Sauce, 172
    Tortellini Salad, 143
    Roasted Vegetable Lasagna, 56
    Sausage Ravioli with Brown Butter Sauce, 60
    Spaghetti with Spicy Sausage and Pepper Sauce, 59
    Vavo's Spaghetti and Meatballs, 170

Pasta Sauces
    Homemade Fettuccini with Bolognese, 53
    Sausage Ravioli with Brown Butter Sauce, 60
    Spaghetti with Spicy Sausage and Pepper Sauce, 59

Pasta Tips, 58

Peaches
    Blueberry Peach Crumb Cake, 198

Peanut Butter
    Double Peanut Butter Chocolate, 46
    Peanut Butter Milkshakes, 135

Peanut Butter Milkshakes, 135

Peanuts
    Klingon "Gagh" or Noodles in Peanut Sauce, 152

Peas
    Mushy Peas, 189

Pecan Bars, 146

Pecans
    Pecan Bars, 146

Pie
    Double Flaky Pie Crust, 82
    Sing a Song of Sixpence French Meat Pie, 82

Pie Crust
    Double Flaky Pie Crust, 82

Pineapple
    Hawaiian Cake, 145
    The Generations Cake, 153

Pizza

Basic Pizza Dough, 20
Breakfast Pizza, 23
Fresh from the Garden Pizza Sauce, 21
Make-Your-Own-Pizza Night, 25
Mediterranean Pizza, 23
Multigrain Pizza Dough, 20

Pizza Dough
Basic Pizza Dough, 20
Multigrain Pizza Dough, 20

Pizza Sauce
Fresh from the Garden Pizza Sauce, 21

Plantains
Fried Plantains, 230

Polenta
Polenta-Cherry Cobbler, 211

Polenta-Cherry Cobbler, 211

Pork
Golabki (Stuffed Cabbage Rolls), 131
Mom's Baked Pork Chops, 134
Sing a Song of Sixpence French Meat Pie, 82
Steamed Dumplings, 103

Portuguese
Folar da Pascoa (Easter Bread), 177
Malasadas (Portuguese Fried Dough, 173
Massa Sovado (Portuguese Sweet Bread), 175
Mom's Portuguese Style Oven Roast, 72
My Grandmother's Sour Soup (Caldo Azedo), 72
Portuguese Kale Soup, 164
Portuguese Stuffing, 168

Portuguese Kale Soup, 164

Portuguese Stuffing, 168

Potato
Asparagus, Potato and Onion Omelet, 199

Potato Puree, 215

Potatoes
Carrot Potato Mash, 74
Colcannon, 196
Creamy Potato Leek Soup, 81
My Garlic Mashed Potatoes, 187
Old Faithful Whipped Mashed Potatoes, 133
Potato Puree, 215
Summer Potato Salad, 144
Vavo's Pan Fried Fish and Red Gravy with Stewed Potatoes, 165

Pudding
Heavenly Chocolate Pudding, 136

Pumpkin
Pumpkin Chip Scones, 122
Pumpkin Granola Pancakes, 89
Pumpkin Spice Muffins, 121

Pumpkin Chip Scones, 122

Pumpkin Granola Pancakes, 89

Pumpkin Spice Muffins, 121

R

Raita, a Cool Cucumber Yogurt Sauce, 184

Red Gravy, 165

Rice
Arroz Doce (Rice Pudding), 84
Chicken Fried Rice, 109
Chicken, Shrimp and Scallop Paella, 201
Infused Basmati Rice, 183
Jamaican Rice, 230

Roasted Asparagus Quiche, 116

Roasted Vegetable Lasagna, 56

Romulan Ale, 151

Roquefort
Crisp Pear and Blueberry Salad with Roquef, 213

Rustic Brown Bread, 186

S

Salad Dressings

Back in the Day Wedge Salad with Thousand Island
   Dressing, 129
Greek Salad Dressing, 223

Salads
Back in the Day Wedge Salad with Thousand Island
   Dressing, 129
Caesar's Tableside Salad, 52
Crisp Pear and Blueberry Salad with Roquefort and
   Roquefort and Roquefort and Toast Walnuts,
   213
Ensalada (Spanish Salad), 200
Greek Salad, 222
Tortellini Salad, 143
Summer Potato Salad, 144

Sandwiches
Sausage and Pepper Heros, 31
Sloppy Joe Sliders, 30
The Great BLT with a Kick, 32

Sauces
Caramel Sauce, 190
Chocolate Wine Sauce, 94
Curry Sauce, 182
Klingon "Gagh" or Noodles in Peanut Sauce, 152
My Grandmother's Spaghetti Sauce, 172
Nate's Delicious Dipping Sauce, 103
Raita, a Cool Cucumber Yogurt Sauce, 184
Spinach Feta Turkey Burgers with Green Goddess
   Mayo, 141
Vavo's Pan Fried Fish and Red Gravy with Stewed
   Potatoes, 165

Sausage
Sausage and Pepper Heros, 31
Sausage Lentil Soup, 208
Sausage Ravioli with Brown Butter Sauce, 60
Spaghetti with Spicy Sausage and Pepper Sauce, 59

Sausage and Pepper Heros, 31

Sausage Lentil Soup, 208

Sausage Ravioli with Brown Butter Sauce, 60

Scallop
Chicken, Shrimp and Scallop Paella, 201

Scones
Pumpkin Chip Scones, 122
Strawberries and Cream Scones, 119
Traditional Irish Scones, 197

Seafood
Chicken, Shrimp and Scallop Paella, 201
Vavo's Pan Fried Fish and Red Gravy, 165

Shrimp
Chicken, Shrimp and Scallop Paella, 201

Side Dishes
Carrot Potato Mash, 74
Cavatappi with Tomatoes and Garlic, 210
Chicken Fried Rice, 109
Colcannon, 196
Creamed Corn, 134
Crisp Pear and Blueberry Salad with Roquef, 213
Curry Sauce, 182
Greek Salad, 222
Infused Basmati Rice, 183
Jamaican Rice, 230
Mushy Peas, 189
My Garlic Mashed Potatoes, 187
Portuguese Stuffing, 168
Potato Puree, 215
Raita, a Cool Cucumber Yogurt Sauce, 184
Tabouleh, 222

Side Dishes
Old Faithful Whipped Mashed Potatoes, 133

Sing a Song of Sixpence French Meat Pie, 82

Sloppy Joe Sliders, 30

Snacks
Granola Clusters, 48
Toasted Pita Chips, 219
Trail Mix, 48

Soup

Creamy Potato Leek Soup, 81

My Grandmother's Sour Soup (Caldo Azedo), 72

Portuguese Kale Soup, 164

Warm and Hearty Minestrone Soup, 45

Soups

Creamy Jamaican Squash Soup, 228

Sausage Lentil Soup, 208

Southern Recipes

Green Tomato Spice Cake with Brown, 75

Southern Sweet Tea with a Twist, 47

Southern Sweet Tea with a Twist, 47

Spaghetti with Spicy Sausage and Pepper Sauce, 59

Spanish Flan (Custard), 202

Spanish Recipes

Asparagus, Potato and Onion Omelet, 199

Chicken, Shrimp and Scallop Paella, 201

Ensalada (Spanish Salad), 200

Spanish Flan (Custard), 202

Spice Glaze, 122

Spinach

Chicken and Spinach Spanakopita, 224

Spinach Feta Turkey Burgers with Green Goddess Mayo, 141

Spinach Feta Turkey Burgers with Green Goddess Mayo, 141

Spread the Love Spiced Carrot Marmalade, 43

Spreads

Spread the Love Spiced Carrot Marmalade, 43

Squash

Creamy Jamaican Squash Soup, 228

Steamed Dumplings, 103

Stews

Coq au Vin, 214

Irish Beef Stew, 195

Stories

"Granny's Pineapple Cake", 156

"Mamma's Pecan Pie", 148

A Medieval Murder Mystery Dinner, 78

Chinese Food for Christmas?, 109

Get Me a Man Pie, 138

No one ever really cooks alone..., 15

Strawberries

Strawberries and Cream Scones, 119

Strawberries and Cream Scones, 119

Stuffing

Portuguese Stuffing, 168

Summer Potato Salad, 144

Sweet Potato Pancakes adorned with Spiced Nuts, 96

Sweet Potato Pancakes adorned with Spiced Nuts, 96

Sweet Potatoes

Sweet Potato Pancakes adorned with Spiced Nuts, 96

Sweet Tea

Southern Sweet Tea with a Twist, 47

T

Tabouleh, 222

The Benefits of a Well Organized Kitchen, 235

The Generations Cake, 153

The Great BLT with a Kick, 32

Tips

COOKIE BAKING TIPS, 38

Helpful Meal Planning and Money Saving Tips, 241

Pasta Tips, 58

The Benefits of a Well Organized Kitchen, 235

Tips for Making Egg Rolls, 106

Tips for Making Egg Rolls, 106

Toasted Pita Chips, 219

Tomatoes

Cavatappi with Tomatoes and Garlic, 210

Traditional Irish Scones, 197

Trail Mix, 48

Turkey
    Cottage Pie with Onion Gravy, 187
    Sloppy Joe Sliders, 30
    Spinach Feta Turkey Burgers with Green Goddess Mayo, 141
    Warm and Hearty Minestrone Soup, 45

V

Vavo's Pan Fried Fish and Red Gravy with Stewed Potatoes, 165

Vavo's Spaghetti and Meatballs, 170

Vegetables
    Carrot Potato Mash, 74
    Chicken and Vegetable Egg Rolls, 105
    Creamed Corn, 134
    Crisp Pear and Blueberry Salad with Roquefort and Roquefort and Roquefort and Toast Walnuts, 213
    Ensalada (Spanish Salad), 200
    Fresh Lettuce Wraps, 104
    Fried Plantains, 230
    Greek Salad, 222
    Mushy Peas, 189
    Old Faithful Whipped Mashed Potatoes, 133
    Potato Puree, 215

Raita, 184
Roasted Vegetable Lasagna, 56
Tabouleh, 222

W

Warm and Hearty Minestrone Soup, 45

Wholegrain
    Tabouleh, 222

Wholegrain Apple Oat Pancakes, 91

Wholegrain Pan Rolls, 69

Wholegrains
    Granola Clusters, 48
    Pumpkin Granola Pancakes, 89
    Wholegrain Apple Oat Pancakes, 91
    Wholegrain Pan Rolls, 69

Wraps
    Fresh Lettuce Wraps, 104
    The Great BLT with a Kick, 32

Y

Yeast Breads
    Folar da Pascoa (Easter Bread, 177
    Massa Sovado (Portuguese Sweet Bread), 175
    Naan Bread, 180
    Rustic Brown Bread, 186

About the Author

Elise is becoming well-known for her TV cooking segments *"Cooking with Elise"*, her blogging at www.CookingwithElise.com and as Chef Spokesperson for BJ's Wholesale Club.

Elise grew up near Boston in Fall River, Massachusetts. A speech impediment kept Elise from talking until she was about sixteen. Her Portuguese grandmother's kitchen became her refuge. Elise's grandmother taught her to cook with the most important ingredient of all – love.

Elise puts that same love into the meals she creates for her own family, friends or anyone who just happens to walk into her kitchen. At her friends' request, Elise began teaching friends, children and college students how to cook. Now through personal appearances, culinary classes, TV, Internet and her new cookbook, she shares that love with others.

In an amazing transformation, the child-who-never-spoke has become the funny, passionate, outspoken Chef Elise that some are calling the "Portuguese Paula Dean". Elise believes wholeheartedly that cooking together and gathering around the table not only creates memories and makes meals eventful, but connects generations.

Elise lives with her husband, Michael, her two sons, Nathaniel and Alexander and her much-loved cat, Isabel, in Raleigh, North Carolina. Elise's favorite food is ice cream!

Made in the USA
Columbia, SC
05 April 2025

56124156R00141